BODY PACKAGING

A Guide to Human Sexual Display

Julian Robinson DesRCA., FRSA

A Guide to Human Sexual Display

PACKAGING

Julian Robinson Des RCA., FRSA.

ELYSIUM Growth Press

A WATERMARK PRESS BOOK

BODY PACKAGING
was created and produced by
The Watermark Press, Sydney

Published in the USA by
ELYSIUM Growth Press, 5436 Fernwood Avenue,
Los Angeles, CA. 90027

Library of Congress Cataloging in Publication Data:

    Robinson, Julian.
           Body packaging: a guide to human
      sexual display/by Julian Robinson.
      p. cm.
      Bibliography: p.
      Includes index.
      ISBN 1-555-99027-4
      1. Costume — Social aspects. 2. Costume
      design — History. 3. Sex customs. 4. Sex
      symbolism. I. Title.
      GT525.R63 1988
      391-dc19

Editor: Alexandra Towle
Assistant editors: Camilla Sandell, Carol Varley
Editorial assistants: Gwen Ormiston, Crispin Blackall

Design: Nicholson Art Direction
Design assistant: Carol Varley
Production coordinators: James Somerled, Claud Parsons

Illustrated letters by Anna Wojak
Index by Michael Wyatt

Typeset by Sabagraphics, New Zealand and Keyset
Phototype, Sydney
Printed by Mandarin Offset, Hong Kong

I dedicate this book to the Chairman and Principal of the Sydney College of the Arts for their generous financial settlement that made this book possible, and to all of those students who faithfully stood by me during my time of trauma when I was fighting in the courts to be allowed to lecture them on this particular subject. Also to all those other students from around the world that it has been my good fortune to meet and advise during the past thirty-five years, and who prompted me to explore this subject more thoroughly than I would otherwise have done. And finally to my three children, Charlotte, Xavier and Georgina, together with my friend Zazimova, without whose help and encouragement I would never have finished this volume. To you all I am extremely grateful.

Contents

Introduction

Every morning, as we prepare ourselves to meet the world, we perform a universal and time-honoured ritual: we change our natural naked state by adding some form of adornment or body covering. This may mean putting on a simple cotton dress, a T-shirt and shorts, a formal business suit, the robes of office of a monarch, or a few daubs of paint. The desire to change our bodies in some way is so universal that it would appear to be an inborn expression of our "humanness"; a trait which sets us apart from the animal world.

However, zoologists tell us that humans are not the only animals who seek to adorn or cover their bodies. Hermit crabs choose to wear discarded shells. There are fish that exude a glue-like substance to which sand and seaweed stick. Some species of dragonfly larva cover their bodies with bits of twig, bark and other oddments which they attach to their bodies with silken threads. There are many species of monkey and ape who seem to gain positive pleasure from self-adornment. So it is possible that the sense of heightened body consciousness we derive from clothing may well be deeply rooted in our psyche. In fact, the physical pleasure we derive from wearing clothes as a fulfillment of this inborn trait could be one of the reasons why we continue to dress ourselves in multitudinous layers of clothing in this technological age of central heating and air conditioning.

It is also important to note that many members of our primate family have evolved very explicit markings on various parts of their bodies for the sole purpose of drawing attention to their sexual characteristics. Sometimes the male genitalia is echoed in the face of a primate species, as in the male mandrill, whose facial features exactly mirror the shape and colouration of his penis and scrotum. Sometimes the female genital region is highlighted, as with the gelada baboon, whose vaginal opening is surrounded by folds of brightly-coloured skin which become engorged and vibrant at the time of ovulation. As the gelada baboon has continued to evolve, the species has adopted a semi-squatting posture, and the female's primary area of sexual display has thus disappeared from general view. To compensate for this loss, a secondary area of sexual display has evolved on the front of the female's body which has similar pinkish-red skin to that of her vulva, and it is no coincidence that this area is also bordered by white papillae with a mimic of the vulva at the centre, created by the bright red nipples of the breasts. You will not be surprised to learn that this chest display increases and decreases in intensity in tune with the changes in the genital region.

The human species has also evolved a system of secondary sexual signalling. The female mimics her primary sexual areas — her genitalia and her rump — on the front of her body and her face. The facial lips, especially when highlighted with cosmetics, resemble the inner lips of the vulva. The breasts, especially when uplifted and padded, resemble the rounded form of the buttocks. The more protuberant male nose is seen as a penis echo, and phallic symbolism and discreet padding are often incorporated into his mode of dress to give an impression of greater bulk, masculinity and virility.

One only has to look through the pages of this book at the enormous number of devices people have employed throughout the ages to draw attention to their sexuality, to conclude that clothing and other forms of body decoration were never designed to conceal, or even to protect the body from the wear and tear of everyday life, but were primarily intended to render the body more sexually attractive.

—

Clothing the Psyche

▲ *"The tendency of beauty of clothing to be accepted as a substitute for beauty of body appeared very early in the history of mankind."* *Havelock Ellis 1905 Studies in the Psychology of Sex Vol. IV*

It would seem that we are ashamed of the naked body with which we were born, just as we seem to be ashamed of many of our bodily functions. Whether the practice of concealing our bodies in multitudinous layers of clothing is the cause of this shame, or whether an inherent prurience is behind the desire for concealment, is not clear. But many authorities on the subject of dress believe that the western obsession with covering every part of the body with some form of clothing is only a passing phase and we may, at some future time, come to accept nakedness as the most desirable form of body packaging.

NAKED AS NATURE INTENDED?

All humans start life completely naked whether they are born in a remote area of the Amazon jungle, the middle of the Sahara desert, deep in the arctic regions of the northern hemisphere or in a modern maternity hospital in an industrialized western country.

When compared with the myriad animals with whom we share this planet, the naked human is a rather uninspiring, puny-looking creature. We have no exotic feathers to display or scales, fangs or claws with which to protect ourselves. And we alone among the 193 species of primate — the group of mammals which includes the monkeys, the apes, the baboons and us — lack even their coat of protective fur.

▲ Regardless of our sex, education, wealth, race or religion we all come into this world stark naked

▲ The vibrant rump region of the female chacma baboon becomes an absolutely irresistible sexual signal during the most fertile period of her menstrual cycle

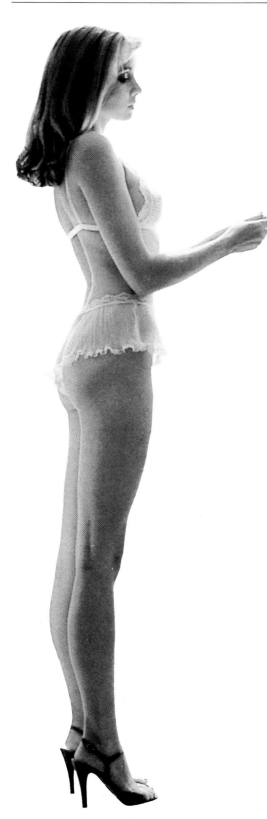

▲ In the west we have become accustomed to wearing a wide variety of garments to make us appear taller, wealthier, prettier, younger and sexier

▶ The male nose has long been seen as an outward and visible symbol of the penis with the tie acting as a penis echo (Painting by Barbara Millet)

HOW HUMANS LOST THEIR FUR

Exactly why our naked bodies lack a natural fur-like covering nobody is quite sure, but most anthropologists believe that at some time during our evolution, natural selection must have favoured nakedness. Some have speculated that when our ancestors were hunter/gatherers, a less hairy body was an advantage, allowing them to run faster when chasing game on the savannah; the insulating hair gradually being replaced by body fat and sweat glands.

Charles Darwin on the other hand proposed that our ancestors "lost their coat of hair for aesthetic reasons, with the members of one sex choosing as mates those of the other sex who were least hairy". Both Desmond Morris and Helen E. Fisher support this view, and in her book *The Sex Contract* (1982) Dr Fisher states that the loss of our main areas of body hair had a distinct advantage for the continued procreation of the species. "With the evolution of hairlessness, the soft delicate areas of the neck, underarm, abdomen and legs became exposed" which, she said, "enabled partners to signal their

desires, to express their excitement, to arouse each other with touch and sight" — a tremendous advantage at a time when sexual bonding had become important for survival.

Dr Fisher also explains why our ancestors didn't lose all their visible hair, and why what they retained appears as well planned as what they lost. The hair that appeared at puberty around the genitals, under the arms and on the male face and chest, signalled sexual maturity.

THE BODY BEAUTIFUL

For whatever reason a naked skin may have appealed to our ancestors back in those primeval days, the vast majority of the human race have now all but abandoned the naked condition. Why should this be?

Do we wear clothes in order to keep out the cold? Charles Darwin pointed out in his journal made during the epic voyage around the world in *HMS Beagle* that he had come across many people in cold climates in the southern hemisphere who did not use any form of body covering to keep themselves warm,

▲ This young girl is making some very clear statements. The colour of the beads and the patterning of the beadwork indicate her unmarried state, and the fact that she is a member of the Mabaso clan, living in a village north of Tugela Ferry, South Africa

◀ Cultural attitudes towards clothing and body decoration differ widely throughout the world with the younger members of each community learning to accept the styles which are traditional within their cultural group as being quite normal, rational and natural

One had as good be out of the world, as out of fashion.
Colley Cibber *1696*

or even to protect themselves from ice and snow, although he recorded that they were rarely unadorned. Generally such adornments were used to denote their tribe and their rank. Numerous other world travellers, both before and since have made similar observations. And even if our blood has thinned over the years, making modern man more susceptible to changes of temperature, it would be *possible* in an age of central heating to go naked. But still we do not.

Do we wear clothes through an inborn sense of modesty? That would not appear to be the whole answer either. The wearing of clothing has become the accepted tradition and walking around in the nude would indeed be very humiliating for most individuals. A naked, or near-naked state would be regarded as immoral or at the very least sexually provocative. But in the Nuba villages of the Sudan, the Mato Grosso region of Brazil, the Highlands of New Guinea or the Maasai villages in Tanzania and Kenya, people do not have this problem. Although they do wear a wide variety of body coverings and adornments, their ideas of modesty differ quite dramatically from our own. In fact, most of their forms of body covering are aimed at drawing attention to the very erogenous zones which we are most concerned with concealing.

DRAWING ATTENTION TO OURSELVES

While some people today may well use their clothing to keep warm and to protect themselves, it would be a mistake to believe that the original function of clothing was in any way connected with such utilitarian functions. It is far more likely that our clothing developed for quite a different reason.

Most anthropologists have suggested that the original purpose of clothing was to draw attention to the erogenous zones. But time and some long-forgotten rituals have gradually transformed attention-seeking garb into a form of concealment. Thus it can be fairly argued that our current modesty about our bodies is the *result* and not the *cause* of our present mode of dressing. Given a more open and understanding cultural education, the embarrassment we now feel about displaying our naked bodies would soon disappear.

The ultimate image of a civilization is its dress.
Paco Rabanne *1980*

◀ *Tribal peoples of the remoter regions of the world spend a great deal of their time decorating and adorning their bodies in order to make themselves look sexually attractive*

▲ *In Japan it is traditional for women to spend a great deal of time and money on packaging their bodies in the style of their ancestors, but recently much of this ancient ritual has been replaced by western concepts of fashion and glamour*

▲ *The ancient Picts who inhabited the British Isles at the time of the Roman occupation were said to have worn nothing more than a decorative covering of wood, and coloured tattoos, but it is doubtful that their body decoration was as skilfully executed as in this idealised portrait of 1804*

▲ *Young people in the west learn about the necessity for dress at a very early age through an elaborate process of punishment and cultural indoctrination*

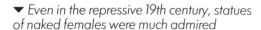

▼ *Even in the repressive 19th century, statues of naked females were much admired*

A NAKED HERITAGE

The fact that we still openly admire the naked body and have idealised it in painting and sculpture shows that nakedness is still an accepted part of our cultural heritage. But in our complex society it has become necessary to cover our naked bodies on almost all social occasions. Nevertheless, the natural desire to decorate ourselves for sexual display is the most important reason for many of today's more adventurous clothing styles, with our clothing serving to heighten our body awareness and sensuality.

The overwhelming majority of people throughout the world, even those living in the most remote areas, would appear to share a predisposition for adorning and decorating their bodies. This indicates that the desire to package and present our bodies attractively is an established human trait. Possibly the forces of natural selection developed this particular predisposition during the latter part of our evolution, a time which has seen the human race multiply from less than 1 million people at the end of the Ice Age to almost 6 billion people today.

Whether the human race can afford to continue to multiply at this rate is an open question. It would seem sensible for the procreative urge to slow down. This could well lead not to further concealment of the body, as most people would expect, but to a dramatic swing back to an honest acceptance of nudity.

Few words in our vocabulary are as loaded, few have been so transformed both as to semantics and to philosophy, few carry such extremes of utter dismissal and ecstatic pursuit, few words match the social richness of 'fashion'.

Toni del Renzio *1975*

THE ORIGINS OF CLOTHES

As if in compensation for our rather lacklustre bodies, we have been given a brain to devise and make many exotic and diverse forms of body covering: these have enabled members of our species to climb the highest mountains, dive to the greatest depths of the ocean, travel at four times the speed of sound and even walk on the surface of the moon. Apart from this practical aspect, we also make body coverings and adornments which give us a special feeling of luxury, make us feel sexy and look younger or taller, learned, religious, wealthy or powerful.

Children learn at every stage of their development that it is by means of clothing that they can identify others and themselves. We identify ourselves as members of our particular society by assuming its mode of dress. Because of the obvious social importance of this convention many writers have gone so far as to suggest that it is possible to chart our ancestors' religious convictions, political mood, moral code, social mores, scientific progress, artistic development and the health of their commerce by what they wore. This is why the genealogy of western clothing styles, once the exclusive province of the costume archivist, today receives the rapt attention of the sociologist, psychologist, anthropologist, economist, art historian and political scientist.

THE FIRST PRACTICAL GARMENT

Many anthropologists believe that the wearing of some form of body covering first evolved during our primeval hunter/

▲ The Greeks admired nakedness and celebrated the act of procreation in their art

▲▲ In almost every known cultural group, superior social position has been clearly marked by the wearing of some form of specialised clothing

gatherer phase of evolution around 500,000 years ago. As our ancestors had to travel considerable distances in the course of a day, they would wear a simple hip or shoulder wrap made from a tied animal skin and tuck their flint tools and weapons into it. Over many millennia this simple innovation would probably have developed into more elaborate and specialized forms of carrying devices; to transport a baby, to collect fruit, roots and seeds or, possibly, a sling to carry the carcass of a freshly-killed animal, or a cover for protecting the genital region which would have been particularly vulnerable in the wild undergrowth.

SOCIAL RANK

Excavations in Mesopotamia reveal that the people who settled around the banks of the Tigris and the Euphrates did not require clothing for warmth, although they did utilize various modes of dress for a variety of other reasons, including the need to distinguish rank and social position and to arouse the sexual desires of their peers. Similarly the early Egyptians, who settled along the fertile banks of the Nile, used clothing to distinguish their leading citizens from the mass of the population. We learn from their detailed hieroglyphics that, although the vast majority of people were either naked or wore

▲ *Ancient Egyptian royalty wore clothing of transparent silk to signal their high status whilst concubines, musicians and dancers glorified in their near-nakedness*

▼ *The Venus of Lespugue and numerous cave paintings from the same era indicate that before 25,000BC some quite complex garments were being worn. As can be seen from this statuette the hip fringe was in no way intended to conceal the shape of the body — on the contrary, it seems to have been worn to draw attention to the fullness of the figure it adorned*

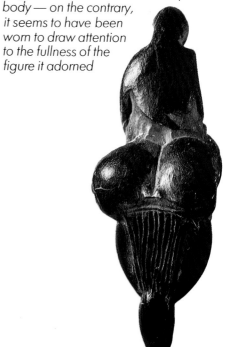

only the most meagre covering, the majority of wealthy Egyptians wore an oblong piece of plain cloth called a *haik* which was draped around the wearer's head and body, primarily as a sign of social status. Ornate and decorative *haik* were reserved by law for high-ranking officials, and only members of the royal family were allowed to wear the more expensive fringed *haik*, or a *kalasiris* which is believed to have been made from a transparent silk imported from China.

The ancient Hittites and Minoans also wore clothing designed to distinguish rank and social position, rather than for any utilitarian purpose. And so did the Greeks and the Romans who, according to such writers as Aristophanes and Juvenal, also looked to their clothing to add allure to their bodies. They certainly didn't want the lower social orders to share their fun, so they protected the rights of the elite to wear prestigious and alluring garments by introducing elaborate sumptuary laws.

MAGIC SYMBOLS

According to cave paintings, carvings and various fragments discovered during the past 250 years, it would appear that the European cave-dwellers of 20-25,000 years ago also used specialised forms of body decoration and adornment as a form of magic symbolism.

Many races of Homo sapiens wore a variety of body decorations and adornments on ceremonial occasions, when hunting and probably during their routine day-to-day lives, to distinguish rank, sexual availability, prowess as a warrior and skill as a hunter. The wearing of the teeth and claws of a predatory animal killed in combat was believed to confer upon the wearer the courage and cunning of the dead animal.

Writers like Hilaire Hiler in *Nudity to Raiment* (1929) suggest that early hunters learnt to wear animal skins as a disguise in order to get nearer to wild herds. In time, this may have led to the association of the wearing of skins with magical powers, and then to ritualistic ceremonies in which the animal skin itself became a magic symbol. This symbolism lives on in the popular subconscious even today. Other decorations and adornments were probably worn to ward off evil spirits. Unable to understand the workings of microbiology, our ancestors thought that certain ailments were the work of evil spirits and used a variety of amulets and particular forms of body decoration to ward off calamity.

Yet other forms of decoration were believed to have a close

▲ There are many theories on the evolution of the yashmak. After travelling through the deserts of Egypt and India, suffering the dust and the flies I subscribe to the theory that the yashmak was invented out of sheer necessity, giving those who wore it a distinct advantage over the environment. After many millennia, this traditional form of protection from the elements became a magic talisman, a symbol of survival which was absorbed into the Muslim faith as the mark of a true believer

[Top] The hunt was imbued with mysticism. With time, the donning of special hunting garb became part of the magic which has lived on in some forms of garment

connection with primitive forms of religion such as ancestor worship. And it would be reasonable to assume that certain modes of decoration were used during times of celebration, as even today, at festival times, races who are normally unclothed dress up to the hilt.

RITES OF PASSAGE

Generally it is the unmarried young men and women who attempt to set themselves off to the best advantage on festive occasions. Both sexes wear as many rings and trinkets upon their arms, legs, fingers, ankles and ears as is regarded desirable and attractive. In his book *History of Human Marriage* (1921) Westermarck brings forward numerous examples of ethnic modes of adornment "which", he says, "serve to attract attention to the sexual regions of both men and women," and observes that, "the sexual organs were covered during these festivities [which is] found to act as the most powerful obtainable sexual stimulus, as generally the sexual organs are unadorned and pass unnoticed".

Festivities to mark particular stages in the progress of various individuals within a cultural group, such as the onset of puberty or the birth of the first born, often demand more permanent forms of decoration or embellishment in the form of tattooing or scarification.

Marking the sexual development of an individual with clothing and decoration became a firm tradition within our own society earlier this century, but this practice has been discontinued in recent years. At the onset of puberty, girls would be permitted to use facial make-up and nail varnish, to wear earrings, high-heeled shoes, bras and stockings. Boys would be given their first pair of long trousers and perhaps a wrist watch or some other form of insignia.

GROUP IDENTIFICATION

As the number of humans increased and they spread out from their place of origin, each cultural group developed particular styles of decoration and embellishment to differentiate their members from their neighbours or their enemies. Distinctively broad noses were made broader by the use of boars' tusks or quills. Naturally large lips were made larger with lip plugs. Ears were pierced and elaborately decorated. Necks were stretched with rings. Feet were bound. Legs were shackled. The inner lips of the labia were elongated. The penis was tightly wrapped and decorated. And although each mode of

▲ The Paduang women of Burma wear solid brass neck and ankle rings which are added to from puberty until the birth of their first child, signifying the family's wealth

▲ Hasidic Jews traditionally indicate their religious and cultural commitment sartorially. They wear the traditional bekescher, a coat of silky material, over the kapote, a long black jacket, with black trousers, a sable hat and the schick und zochen, slippers and white knee socks.

▲ These young Maasai girls from the Great Rift Valley of Kenya and Tanzania are rapidly approaching puberty. They have decorated themselves with traditional forms of necklaces, wooden plug-like ear rings and head adornments as a sign of their growing maturity

▼ A young engaged girl from the Hombela clan in South Africa. After marriage the whole mode of her adornments will change to signify her new status

embellishment was quite different, they all served the same purpose: to increase sexual attractiveness.

SEXUAL ALLURE

Many anthropologists now believe that since the invention of the first tool-carrying hip or shoulder wrap, our ancestors gradually discovered that such a device had enormous potential in helping them organize and adjust their natural sexual signalling areas. Gradually a range of adornments were contrived. In some cases they were actually a form of sexual mimicry which echoed, or symbolized, the wearer's natural physical attributes or physiological state.

These sexual signalling devices are still very much with us today, ranging from the elongated gourd penis sheaths worn by the Highland warriors of New Guinea to the overt figure-hugging jeans and T-shirts worn by the nubile young of western

▲ ▶ *Many forms of western clothing are specifically intended to stimulate the imagination of the onlooker with the merest glimpse of a partly-covered erogenous zone*

▲ *There are many places in the world where it is the accepted custom to display and even to highlight the genitalia of the sexually-active members of the community*

society. Most sartorial experts agree that clothing that covers yet displays the gender of the wearer transmits a sexual message. But even when our chosen form of body packaging is clearly distinguishable as sexual in nature, it should not necessarily be construed as being sexual in intent.

YOU ARE WHAT YOU WEAR

Of course not all forms of body presentation and packaging are overtly or symbolically sexual in nature. Some are simply intended to denote wealth or social position, cultural origin or form of employment. Some are purely protective, such as those worn when scuba diving, smelting metals, mountaineering or when sterile conditions are required, such as in an operating theatre. Others act as a disguise by transforming the wearer into a demon or a deity. But these dress forms are very specific and, although they do not make a point of emphasising the erogenous zones of the wearer, they are invariably worn with a secondary layer of underclothing. This is concealed from view but reassures the wearer of their gender.

People tend to clothe their psyche as much as their bodies,

wearing whatever makes them feel younger, richer, more intelligent, artistic, rebellious, athletic, or whatever suits the personal image they are trying to promote.

Professor Flugel in *The Psychology of Clothes* (1929) went to great lengths to list a wide variety of secondary motives for wearing clothes, some of which have been mentioned earlier, but are nevertheless worthy of listing once again: *sign of rank, locality and nationality, display of wealth, extension of bodily self, occupation, modesty and protection, expression of individual differences, sex distinction* and a form of *trophism*. Other writers have extended this list to include: *magic, defence against the evil eye,* varying *aesthetic* reasons and *matrimonial possession.* However, Professor Flugel makes it very clear that it has been "manifest to all serious students of dress that of all the motives for the wearing of clothes, those connected with the sexual life have an altogether predominant position." And he concludes: "clothing originated largely through the desire to enhance the sexual attractiveness of the wearer and to draw attention to the genital organs of the body."

▲ Protective clothing, such as that worn by airport fire fighters, is purely functional, but under this outward packaging most fire operatives wear undergarments which reassure them of their gender and individuality

▼ Certain forms of body packaging are worn in order to totally transform the wearer into a different kind of being. They are clothing the psyche rather than the body

Other authors may well argue that clothing is chosen to display a variety of information about the wearer, for protection or other utilitarian purposes. However, I know from my own experience as a fashion designer and as a costume historian, that the vast majority of people still wish to make the most of their more attractive and desirable physical attributes, and to display these to advantage. Many of these individuals may be blissfully unaware of the sexual signals their clothing styles display, but coded sexual messages are nevertheless an important ingredient in their choice of garments. In fact, these coded messages are the very reason we like or dislike many of the styles we wear or see.

CHANEL
BOUTIQUE

26 OLD BOND STREET · LONDON W1

▲ Throughout history wealth and social position has always been a sexual excitant for both men and women, so it is little wonder that many people today use an obviously expensive style of dress to increase their sex appeal

THE ORIGINS OF MODESTY

"In the Garden of Eden, our first parents, Adam and Eve, did take the apple from the serpent. They did both eat of it, and then they perceived that they were naked and that it was shameful to be so. They did make themselves aprons of fig leaves in order to hide the cause of their shame from the eyes of the Lord".

An Abridgement of Scripture History for Children, (1765).

Apart from enjoying the authority of biblical tradition, few authorities on matters of dress support the notion that modesty is in any way connected with the origins of clothing. On the contrary, most ancient cultures accepted nudity as a normal part of everyday life.

FAMILIARITY BREEDS ACCEPTANCE

In ancient Greece nakedness was openly accepted, particularly when dancing or performing gymnastic feats. Plato, in *The Republic*, approved of such customs. He advocated the free association of naked boys and girls in part to blunt the edge of normal pubescent sexual appetites.

Modesty is, in fact, a fairly recent innovation in the western world and is the *result* rather than the *cause* of wearing clothing. In volume 1 of *Studies in the Psychology of Sex* (1901) Havelock Ellis advances the view that it was the Romans, showing "no perception of the moralizing and refining influence of nakedness", who laid the foundations of what he described as "Christian morality". Once the Romans were converted to Christianity the ecclesiastics began to identify the notion of nakedness as the work of the devil and to connect it with original sin. Thus modesty, as we now know it, was born.

▲ Our society has great difficulty in perceiving the naked male body as being beautiful. This is a form of distorted sexism based on the belief that there are parts of the male body which are inherently obscene. The Ancient Greeks had an altogether different attitude as this 6th century BC statuette of Silenus clearly shows

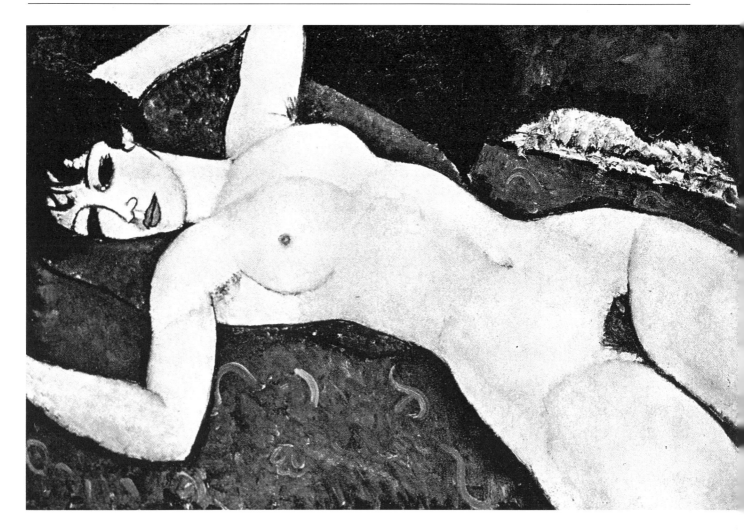

FIGHTING 'THE FLESH'

Despite the fact that these early Christians had found so many of Plato's opinions congenial, they would have nothing to do with his liberal views on nakedness. As Havelock Ellis clearly puts it: "they failed to recognize its psychological correctness. The reason was simple, and indeed simple-minded. The Church was passionately eager to fight against what it called 'the flesh' and thus fell into the error of confusing the subjective question of sexual desire with the objective spectacle of the naked form. 'The flesh' is evil; therefore, 'the flesh' must be hidden. And they hid it, without understanding that in so doing they had not suppressed the craving for the human form but, on the contrary, had heightened it by imparting to it the additional fascination of a forbidden mystery."

The new religious leaders had, in fact, become obsessed with the new notion of modesty. But, powerless to actually spirit away human sexuality, generation after generation of church leaders sought to legislate against the open display of all forms of gender display, both in clothing and in pictorial representations of the human form. Religious edicts ordered the

▲ ▼ Painters depict the most admired feminine form of their day. Above is a work by Modigliani dated 1917, and below a medieval academic painting by Cranach the Elder

◀ ▲ *The history of women's fashions has been one based on a continual round of changing erogenous zones, a theory first put forward by Professor J C Flugel of the Department of Psychology in the University of London and author of the Psychology of Clothes (1929). He is of the opinion that we tend to regard clothes from two incompatible points of view — on the one hand as a means of displaying our physical attributes; on the other hand as a means of hiding our shame. And he went on to compare western clothes to "a perpetual blush upon the surface of humanity" — a blush, I might add, that exaggerates the normal symptoms of shame thereby gratifying our unconscious desire for exhibitionism, thus adding enchantment and mystery to our way of life that would not otherwise exist*

sculptured effigies of men to be castrated and the pubic region of women to be rendered smooth. In paintings and anatomical drawings the offending male penis and female pubic hair were omitted altogether in order to conform to prevailing ideals of religious *wholesomeness.*

Concealment is food for the inquisitive.
Herbert Ward *1895*

MODESTY BREEDS DESIRE
The clothing styles of the lower echelons of the congregation were made to conform to a very strict moral code, intended to enforce the concealment of as many of the gender signalling areas as possible. A situation was therefore created whereby many of the faithful actually became ashamed and embarrassed by their naked God-given bodies. The upper strata of society took little notice of such religious edicts, except to make sure that the lower orders conformed, in order to set themselves apart with a touch of fashionable sinfulness.

Women's world is the universe of appearance. Costume, style, shape, colour, taste, detail — a woman manipulates these to wrest power and prestige from other women. If fashion is frivolous, dress for women is domination.
Gina Lurie *1976*

But things did not turn out as planned. Many females found that the very act of concealment excited a greater interest among members of the opposite sex, thus creating exactly the opposite effect to that intended by the religious leaders. And so it was that feminine modesty became established throughout the western world. On this particular point Elizabeth B Hurlock eloquently states in *The Psychology of Dress* (1929) that: "it is unquestionably a well-known fact that familiar things arouse no curiosity, while concealment lends enchantment and stimulates curiosity . . . a draped figure with just enough covering to suggest the outline, is far more alluring than a totally naked body." She later adds that ornament and clothing "call attention to the parts of the female body which otherwise would go unnoticed . . . the necessity for this artificial stimulation was to be found in the fact that the male is often apathetic while the female is naturally coquettish." Many writers have explored this intriguingly overt sexual role of modesty: the general hypothesis is that it is only possible to be immodest once an accepted form of modesty has been established.

Theorists have spoken of places in the world where it is the general custom to go naked and "only harlots wear clothes, the covering acting as a sexual lure." Others mention that in the western world "parts of the body are hidden in order to be shown," and have pointed out that "modesty in dress renders lovers more ardent."

It would seem therefore that modesty is, to say the least, ambivalent in that it allows us to satisfy simultaneously two contradictory tendencies in our mode of dress and our behaviour. On one hand, the western form of modesty requires particular parts of the human body to be covered whilst in the company of members of the opposite sex, but on the other hand we know that the very act of covering these parts draws attention to them.

▲ ▲ ▼ *Sensuous fabrics, tightly-laced corsets, tight jeans and high heels all serve to heighten body awareness and stimulate the wearer's sexual appetite, causing them to project a high degree of sexual allure*

THE HIDDEN BONUS

This enforced covering of the body made many individuals acutely aware of their physical selves and they found that by wearing an assortment of garments that rubbed against parts of their bodies they experienced varying degrees of sexual excitement which added to their outward allure. Havelock Ellis mentions several women of his acquaintance who regularly received sexual pleasure from the rhythmic movement created within the labia whilst out walking or attending a dance

▲ Before the days of lingerie female genitals were frequently displayed, as this drawing by Thomas Rowlandson shows

▲ In common with many other women, Queen Elizabeth II subconsciously wears buttoned pocket flaps, the buttons positioned to act as nipple mimics

wearing a tightly-laced corset and high-heeled shoes. Although this did not always lead to orgasm, these ladies confided to Ellis: "it makes one feel quite ready for it."

Florenz Ziegfeld was also aware of the ability of lingerie to physically excite the young chorus girls employed in his famous *Ziegfeld Follies* in the 1920s. He insisted that the girls wear loosely-cut silk cami-knickers which gently stroked the inside of their thighs, so that their faces and bodies would project a state of sexual excitement and appear particularly vibrant and appealing.

This phenomenon of sexual recompense created by the wearing of various forms of clothing was a remarkable incentive for our ancestors to acquiesce to the church's demand for concealment; particularly with the additional bonus of heightened sexual awareness. It can be seen, therefore, that modesty is so intertwined with sexual desire and the need for sexual display — fighting but at the same time re-kindling this desire — that a self-perpetuating process is inevitably set in motion. In fact modesty can never really attain its ultimate end except through its own disappearance. Hiding under the cloak of modesty there are to be found many essential components of the sexual urge itself, without which our sexual appetites would greatly diminish.

HUMAN SEXUALITY

Modern research has shown that human beings are without doubt the sexual athletes of the animal kingdom. Unlike most other animals, which tend to copulate only during a particular season when the females are ovulating, the majority of adult humans are constantly on the prowl. In fact, most anthropologists believe that being sexually aggressive was essential for human development, and that our proto-hominoid ancestors were possibly even more sexually orientated than we are today.

Dr Helen Fisher goes into great detail in *The Sex Contract* to explain why this should be so. It appears that at first these primeval ancestors lived without any form of pair bonding, with the females rearing their young as best they could. As life became more complex, the over-burdened females began looking around for help.

This was a crucial stage in human development. Dr Fisher explains how the more sexually-active proto-hominoid mothers gradually realised that "everywhere was an untapped work force, a cornucopia, a gold mine — proto-hominoid males." They needed only to woo these males into helping them, and their

▲ *The bra-less model is fully aware of her nipple display and all that it implies*

young would survive. During this developmental period most females were sexually active only during ovulation. However, some females were far more sexually active than was the norm, being willing to receive the sexual attentions of males throughout their monthly cycle, during pregnancy, and whilst breastfeeding their young. By about 5 million years ago, these amorous females and their infants had acquired the enormous advantages of protection and a plentiful supply of food. The offspring of these mothers had a far better chance of survival than the infants of less sexually-active mothers.

Dr Fisher believes that "more of the infants of sexier mothers did live, grow up, and breed — passing this genetic anomaly to a greater percentage of the next generation." Natural selection had begun to favour the sexier female.

IT PAYS TO ADVERTISE

Today we signal our sexuality with an elaborate combination of gestures, clothing styles, ornamentation and varying forms of body decorations; sending a continual stream of coded sexual

▼ *In the Kama Sutra lovers were advised to adorn themselves with perfume and jewellery to add interest to their love making*

invitations to members of the opposite sex. However, in order to avoid stimulating the sexual instincts of members of one's own sex, we have gone to great lengths over the years to establish a clear sexual difference in dress. Coming from promiscuous stock we are, as Professor Flugel pointed out, "all potentially ambisexual in our inclinations . . . and the possibility of regression to the ambisexual stage (or even, in the case of many, to a stage at which homosexuality predominated) is always present. One way of guarding against this regression is a somewhat exaggerated or obsessive insistence upon heterosexuality."

Mistakes in sexual signalling are best avoided by a clear differentiation of clothing styles and it is on this double basis — the desire to guard against the possibility of homosexual advances and the inbuilt urge to stimulate the interest of members of the opposite sex into a sexual union — that our current distinction in dress is based.

WHAT ARE THE FORCES OF CHANGE?

Throughout recorded history both men and women have been willing to go to enormous lengths to change their physical appearance to be what we term "fashionable".

▲ One of the primary reasons for changes in women's clothing styles is determined by the need to maintain men's sexual interest. This can be best achieved by transferring the primary area of erotic display from one area to another. The novelty value of this system would soon wane if the central feature of erotic interest was openly flaunted, so this area is generally kept covered up

◀▲ Fashion imagery itself has created the climate for change in our clothing styles. This was particularly true in the 1920s when fashion illustrators like Charles Martin (left) greatly influenced the prevailing mode and helped to change the moral outlook of the times. Attitudes towards the open display of breasts was further eased by pin-ups which were published during the height of World War II to ease the pervading tension

▲ *Maintaining the body beautiful requires discipline and hard work*

SUFFER TO BE BEAUTIFUL

Each change of fashion would bring forth howls of protest from religious leaders, philosophers, law-makers and the like. But far from being put off, people were prepared to suffer not only the displeasure of the law-makers, but a great deal of physical discomfort. Consider the pain caused by wearing shoes which are too tight or too high; the misery of a body distorted by steel and whalebone corsets; the tortuous process of running a feather through the septum of the nose; the agony caused by scarification and tattooing, or malforming the lips, filing teeth, removing the foreskin or the clitoris.

All attest to the powerful human need to conform to the ideals of a current trend, and to be seen to be part of a cultural wholesomeness. But why does this need exist?

TRIBAL MARKS

People's actual physical form changes from one area to the next as do their culture, traditions, ideals and aspirations. On my travels round the world, for instance, I found that what was regarded as most attractive about a person in England

▲ ▲ ▲ *To make oneself attractive to a mate, and to be seen to belong to a group, are universal desires which can demand a high degree of suffering and discomfort*

◀ ▲ ▶ Monarchs and chieftains are marked as special by their clothes and their trappings, with these being accepted as symbols of their unquestioned authority

◀ ◀ ▲ Varying cultural groups mark out their differences from one another in innumerable ways, ranging from teeth filing to specific scar patterning in order to achieve what they see as a socially acceptable body

may be seen as ugly in Japan. And what was pleasing about a person in Japan was often considered hideous in parts of Africa. And what was considered beautiful about a person in Africa somehow seemed less appealing to those who lived in Peru. And what was considered agreeable about a person in Peru was thought to be displeasing in parts of North America. Yet in their countries of origin there was little dispute about their attractive qualities.

I soon came to realize that there is a natural tendency for all people to think of those from their own society as the most appealing and generally the most beautiful. And people tend to accentuate the particular characteristics which set them apart from neighbouring peoples.

The ancient Greeks, who were by no means prudish when it came to the enjoyment of the flesh, plucked out their sparse pubic hair because it did not conform to their aesthetic ideals. The Chinese for many hundreds of years bound their already small feet to make them even smaller — a technique also practised in parts of Europe among aristocratic women during the early Middle Ages. Some races with broad heads, broadened the heads of their babies with a special form of binding.

In the western world today vast numbers of men and women undergo various forms of plastic surgery to re-shape their noses, lift a double chin, remove part of their intestines so they have a flatter stomach, or improve upon the shape of their breasts, buttocks or scrotum with silicone implants. The vast majority of men also shave to remove their facial hair whilst women do the same to their underarms, legs and around what is coyly known as their bikini line. All in the name of a "standardized" concept of beauty.

But Darwin, in *The Descent of Man* (1871) scoffed at the notion that there was any form of standardized human beauty. "It is certainly not true," he wrote, "that there is in the mind of man any universal standard of beauty," and if any such standard was invented, he said, "we would for a time be charmed; but we should soon wish for variety; and as soon as we had obtained variety, we should wish to see certain characteristics a little exaggerated beyond the then existing standards." In this, as in so many of his other perceptions of the human species, Darwin was absolutely right. For although the various members of each cultural group have striking similarities, there are also interesting divergences which allow members of the opposite sex to find someone within the group who conforms to their imagined ideal or their

Human nature is very complex, very mysterious, and often very perverse — our clothing styles certainly mirror this.
Prof. Janey Ironside *1975*

In order to attract mates or paramours, people in every corner of the world have made extraordinary efforts to look sexy.
Dr Helen E Fisher *The Sex Contract, 1982*

▲ *Children learn the rituals of tribal decoration at their mother's knee*

particular fetish. In fact many authorities have claimed that fetishism and disparity are the main influencing factors when choosing a partner.

WEALTH AND POWER

Once clothing had become firmly established as a form of decoration and adornment, those in power sought to reserve certain forms of clothing styles for themselves, so that the elite would be instantly recognized and respected.

Great rivalry existed within this privileged group, with each member trying to out-parade the other. This led to the introduction of an elaborate series of sumptuary laws to control who was allowed to wear what and created a distinct hierarchy of sub-groups. In order to overcome such laws and to gain privileges beyond their station, those who aspired to climb the social ladder werc continually acquiring new styles which had not yet been regulated. Eventually the sumptuary laws were scrapped as it proved impossible to police them. Then a new motivating force became fashionable: money.

▲ *What are meaningless daubs to one group are, to another, specific signals loaded with social and sexual significance*

▼ *Napoleon crowned himself Emperor of France in 1804, and made full use of the symbolism of regalia. People in the west have been programmed to respond to jewelled crowns, scarlet robes and gold embroidery with awe and obedience*

◀▲ *Whatever turns you on. The female ear was at one stage considered to be an outrageously erotic echo of female genitals that every right-thinking woman should hide from view. In the 14th and 15th centuries pregnancy was viewed as a sexy condition, particularly suited to young brides, as seen in this painting of* The Arnolfini Marriage *by Jan Van Eych c. 1454*

▼ *In the late 18th century moralists were complaining bitterly about the vogue for dresses that showed the ankles and the outline of the thighs and breasts*

A wealthy middle class was emerging whose members wished to distinguish themselves from the poorer classes. They chose expensive modes of dress as a system of social segregation. Naturally, those who were most wealthy chose the most expensive. Those who weren't quite as wealthy tried to imitate them. But as soon as a class copied the one above it, the superior class would in turn attempt to achieve greater distinction in their clothing — eventually resulting in a rampant case of conspicuous consumerism.

The interplay of wealth and social position was for a time one of the main motivating forces for change in fashion, but behind these changes was always the desire to be thought "attractive". Not forgetting, of course, that wealth and a highly-regarded social position have always been among the most powerful aphrodisiacs.

STIMULATING DESIRE

The conflict between the desire for concealment and the urge to display was also an important factor in the styles adopted during this period of rapid change. And by far the easiest way

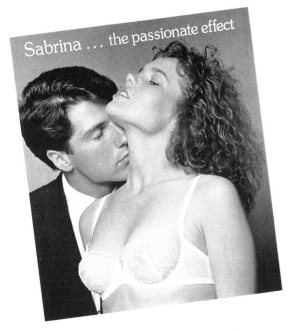

Sabrina ... the passionate effect

▲ ▼ *Thanks to the dressmaker's artifice, we have become accustomed to admire certain physical attributes without ever actually laying eyes upon them*

of stimulating the observer's interest is to display different erogenous zones in different outfits. A little more breast shown in this one, a little more leg in that one, the curve of the buttocks in another: this would guarantee a continuing interest from the opposite sex.

But being a rather conformist society, these erogenous zone displays were orchestrated within each social group. Certain parts of the body would, in their turn, be licensed for exposure and excused as 'the fashion' and therefore become socially acceptable. Thus breasts could be displayed without any feeling of shame as all other breasts in one's social group were also being displayed — but the trick was for each member to make her breasts appear the most attractive. The following season may have seen attention focused on the lower part of the body, clearly delineating the buttock cleavage, or the curve of the thigh. But the intention was always the same: to arouse sexual interest in members of the opposite sex, even if there was no desire to consummate it.

▲ In 1969 'flower power' was at its height
and, circumstances permitting, hippies often
went naked and unashamed

◀ ▲ ▼ *We wear clothes as a cultural badge, to reassure ourselves that we belong to a tribe, and we fondly think that our tribe is somehow better than all the rest. But when it comes to important matters such as choosing a mate, sexual attraction between individuals is often more powerful than cultural ties because under all those layers of invention is the same human animal that has existed for over 50,000 years*

MOSS BROS

Fashion is the mirror of history
Louis XIV

POLITICS

Sometimes fashions change because society itself changes and people's dreams and aspirations change. When this happens people often find that changing the clothes they wear can help them to change themselves into the sort of people they would like to be. They think that by wearing different clothes, they will in fact be different people. But at such times people are also concerned that their dream should not be shared by too many; such 'dreams' are always a matter of 'them' and 'us'. They require a badge of exclusivity. And the moment a fashion becomes truly popular is the moment when it starts to decline. This particular type of fashion change is usually instigated by the young generation who wish to establish their ideological differences. They often deliberately choose a style which would make an older generation look ridiculous or out-of-date.

A SENSE OF BELONGING

Of course not everyone wishes to be a slave to fashion. Many individuals make specific choices, however few have the force of character needed to dress in their own style and ignore the prospect of social disapproval.

Most people, in fact, prefer to keep up with changing trends in order to avoid being disapproved of or labelled as behind the times. The majority also avoid being in the forefront of change for fear of being thought a social rebel. They do however, still purchase far more clothes than they actually need because the act of purchasing new garments reaffirms their membership of a particular society. It states clearly: "I belong".

Belonging to a particular cultural group is a very important ingredient in our ever-changing, fashion-orientated society. It would seem logical to abandon all desire for change as it would be much easier to demonstrate that we 'belong', without having to re-state that fact next year in next year's mode. However, it has been clearly demonstrated that, no matter how strong our urge for stability, we have an equally strong urge for change. This apparent conflict has been solved by orchestrating the desire for change into socially-acceptable fashion trends. 'Fashion' allows us to dress slightly differently from last year, thus satisfying the desire for change and at the same time it allows us to 'belong', to conform with our peer group who are also sporting this year's clothes.

The Historical
Perspective

n all western cultures a system has evolved which allows some gender-signalling areas of the body to be displayed at various times provided the rest are kept covered. This system of shifting sexual emphasis is referred to as the 'changing erogenous zone theory'. Looking back over the past 500 years or so, it is possible to see how the socially imposed rules of modesty based on this theory have varied greatly from one era to the next. The basic principal of 80% concealment, leaving 20% revealed, has remained fairly constant up to the present century.

FROM CODPIECE TO CRAVAT

In a traditionally clothed society such as ours, it is the packaged product which we take for the man or woman. We learn to admire and ardently desire the packaged body. It is the urge to stimulate sexual desire among the opposite sex that would appear to be the main motivating force behind the many extravagant and strange forms of male body packaging from the past.

HARD TIMES
Life in the early Middle Ages — which is when the development of our present mode of dress began — was for most people spartan and monotonous with daily toil following daily toil in dreary succession. For such people a simple body covering of crudely-woven fabric with a sack-like cut and without much

▶ *"An Essay on Women, illustrated with notes from various authors. Invented and drawn by V Green and engraved by I Roberts, London 1769"*

Our choice of clothes, I believe, is not arbitrary, but dictated to us by the deepest unconscious desires of the opposite sex.
James Laver 1973

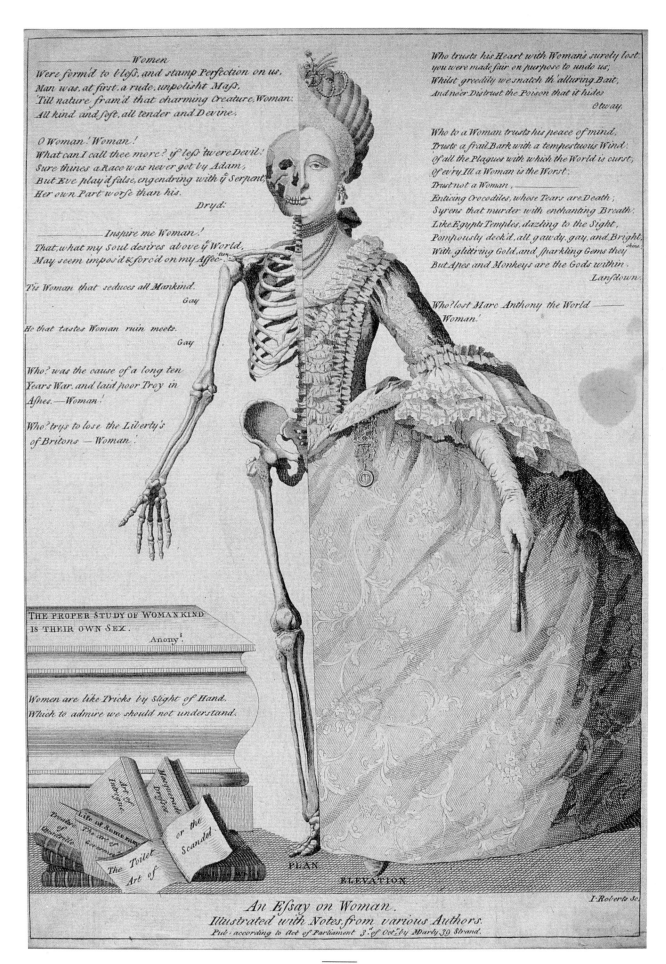

▲ *Venetian courtiers of the 15th and 16th centuries were at the forefront of fashion. This engraving, dated 1590, shows a courtesan wearing a pair of very high chopines*

▲ *Portrait of an Italian courtier, an example of the not-so-subtle codpiece that was fashionable during the Middle Ages*

form or adornment was the sum of their sartorial splendour.

For the ruling class, inheritors of all the arable land as well as all of the wealth, life was a great deal easier. This they displayed in their lifestyle — their homes, their food, their entertainments and their clothes — with both wealth and power aggressively displayed on all occasions.

At the beginning of this period, between the 11th and 12th centuries, the garments worn by members of the ruling class appear to have been both decorative and comfortable. The female dresses were cut long and loose, worn with overgarments trimmed with fur and generally without any underclothing. The male members of this elite society wore a belted tunic and fitted nether-hosen made in two separate sections held together around the waist by a string tie, but they were not joined around the crotch. They also wore a loose-fitting overgarment which was trimmed with fur and worn with imposing pieces of jewellery. Not much sex attraction there, one might reasonably suggest, except that there was already a distinct difference in the dress styles of the sexes which had not existed in Roman times. So at least they knew who was who and what was where.

WANTON TIMES

Within a century of such an inauspicious beginning, the dress styles of our forebears began to blossom with a wide range of provocative styles, many of which would not be allowed today even in the most progressive of western countries.

The high-ranking nobles of Edward IV's court for instance, were permitted to display their naked genitals below a newly-introduced shortened tunic (their tightly-fitting nether-hosen were still left unseamed around the underbody line). If their genitals were not of sufficient size to make a distinguished display, they wore a *braquette* — an explicit glove-like device made of natural skin-coloured leather that was tailored to fit the well-padded penis and scrotum of the wearer.

To preserve the novelty of this form of explicit sexual display, Edward had a law passed in 1348 prohibiting "any knight under the rank of a lord, or any other person " from wearing any gowne, jaket or cloke unless it be of sufficient length on a man standing upright to cover his privy member and buttokkes." The high-ranking nobles could, of course, continue to reveal whatever they pleased, whether or not they were wearing the *braquette* and contemporary reports indicate that this is exactly what they did. Even Chaucer commented upon the continuing use of this male fashion in *The Parson's Tale*, written around 1400. Many men's garments, he wrote, "were horribly scanty — too short to cover their shameful members."

In the 16th century, during the reign of Henry VIII it was fashionable for males of wealth and good social standing to display their manly charms in the finest silken fabrics, bedecked in jewels and lace and sporting a protuberant, padded and embroidered codpiece which greatly enhanced their major sexual feature, in much the same way as some rock stars of the 1970s added padding to their crotch bulge to excite young fans.

Men have also worn whalebone and steel corsets to trim their waistlines and to accentuate their naturally larger chests and shoulders. At other times they have eaten fervently in order to gain body weight, and then added padding to their chests and shoulders to appear more manly, thus increasing their apparent power by sheer size. During the 17th and 18th centuries many men of fashion added thigh and calf pads to the inside of their hosen to enhance the appeal of their masculine legs and padded the front crotch area to simulate a perpetual erection — a most attractive feature for the many women of the royal courts who apparently craved continual sexual indulgence.

Some garments took on the role of a phallic symbol as happened in the 12th and 13th centuries with the long *poulaine* shoe which the Pope described as "the most abominable emblem of immodesty" when he had them banned from his court. They were also prohibited by royal ordinance for their obvious phallic connotations, but those who had the power to flaunt the law continued to wear them. It has been suggested that their main appeal was the extended toe section, which was originally made phallic shaped, but over time it became longer and thinner allowing the wearer to partake in an elaborate form of courtship under the banqueting table by ardently stroking the foot and even the inside of the thighs and the genitals of a young maid sitting opposite him.

THE BEST AVAILABLE CHOICE

It is popularly assumed that women during the Middle Ages were mere chattels with no rights to property and no free choice in marriage. Thomas Wright, in his authoritative book *Womankind in Western Europe* (1869) points out that women of the upper echelons of society were the accepted equals of men and, Wright suggests, "it was the woman who invariably

▲ A Venetian male courtier of the 1590s fashionably hatted and padded around the abdomen and the chest in order to achieve the desired masculine silhouette of the period

▲ A rare illustration showing the long pointed poulaine shoes that were the rage of the Royal courts in the 12th and 13th centuries

▲ Portrait of the Duke of Saxony, 1514, showing how the elaborate fashion for 'slashing', invented by the rich merchant classes was soon copied by the aristocracy and accepted at court

made the first advances to a man of her choice and who conducted the pace of the courtship."

Between the 12th and 18th centuries, the fashionable male made his choice of clothing to please the ladies of the courts and to impress his peers. His opulent clothes put him into a position whereby the women he admired would choose him to breed with — and not the other way round as is so commonly supposed. A man, even in the Middle Ages, could not seize a woman and force her to have his children; instead he put himself in a position whereby he was seen to be the best available choice. One of the best strategies for this was — and incidently still is — to display sexual prowess and wealth in the clothes he wore. And he went to considerable lengths.

Many writers on the period have noted that the women of the courts were often very promiscuous and used numerous beauty aids to enhance their allure and increase their chances of a sexual conquest. It would seem from contemporary accounts that the ladies were however only following the example set by the men. The social commentators and religious preachers of the 12th, 13th and 14th centuries were far more scathing towards the extravagant and sexually-explicit finery of the knights and esquires than they were towards the clothing of the ladies.

SOCIAL STANDING V. MONEY

Until the end of the 14th century the courts of Europe unquestionably ruled the fashion scene. All new styles were introduced by the wealthy and powerful aristocrats, both as a form of novel entertainment and as a means of attracting the attention of members of the opposite sex. During the 15th century, with the growth of international trade with the East,

◀ *Baroque French finery and elaborate wigs designed to entice a suitable partner at the court of Louis XIV*

◀▲▲ *From the Middle Ages through to the 17th century, women of rank were often as politically and socially powerful as the men. Women chose as partners (in marriage and for brief sexual liaisons) the men who presented themselves in the most desirable light, and men vied with one another to display, through their clothing, their fashion-consciousness, their wealth and their masculinity*

REX.   LUDOVICUS   LUDOVICUS REX

"LUDOVICUS REX."

HISTORICAL HAIRDRESSING

Dr Bysterveld edit.   Imp Falconer Paris

La Frégate la Junon
Coiffure Louis XVI

Fig. 353. (13) A Typical Example of the "Historical Fantasia" "Coiffure"
439

▲ *Ludicrous wigs were not the sole preserve of the gentleman*

One fashion has scarcely destroyed another when it is abolished by one yet newer, which in its turn makes way for that which follows it, and it will not be the last.
La Bruyère *1680*

the merchant class began to gain in wealth and power and to display this in their modes of dress.

The European courts responded by introducing a new range of sumptuary laws (laws governing personal habits) which confined various modes of dress, specific fabrics, colours and decorative trims to the members of the court, with those of royal blood being given the sole right to wear the rarest and the most notable. The royal courts also attempted to reserve the right to introduce all new fashions — an impossible task which eventually gave rise to the strange and costly fashion of slashing. Merchants of great wealth in the 16th century would have garments constructed from the most expensive fabric permitted to their station in life. These fabrics were then meticulously slashed and another more expensive fabric — which technically was not part of the construction of the garment — was pulled through the slashing, clearly demonstrating the wearer's fabulous riches without actually breaking the law.

At other times, men of fashion have worn the most elaborately curled hair, long pigtails and powdered wigs. During the 18th century, men of high status had over 110 differently-styled wigs to choose from, the largest being the extraordinary 18-inch/45cm high *Macaroni* which required the hair of at least five other people to make properly. The cost of such a wig was so enormous it could only be afforded by the very wealthy — hence the term *bigwig* today, for an important person.

Prior to the French Revolution, men of fashion also wore a great deal of powder and paint upon their faces. They wore cloaks of office over brightly-coloured velvet coats and embroidered waistcoats, lace trimmings, ruffs, jewellery, fine silk stockings and pantaloons as voluminous as those worn by a harem eunuch.

▲ *This extravagantly-dressed German merchant of the early 16th century clearly speaks of a society that was prosperous enough to employ an army of specialised craftsmen to make every item worn by both man and horse, indicating that the bourgeoisie were on the rise and would soon demand the right to dress as they pleased*

▲ *In the first few years after the French Revolution of 1789, men's fashions became suddenly drab and uninteresting as all the frills and fripperies associated with the aristocracy were speedily discarded in favour of the style of the proletariat pictured here by Boilly*

AN EXTRAVAGANT BREEDING STRATEGY

This extravagance in male dress was extremely successful until the end of the 18th century. The ever-changing array of male apparel projected the right image for the man of inherited social privilege and wealth in the eyes of the women he admired and desired. These fine fashions, with their costly displays of coloured embroidery, jewels, frills, lace and silken stockings were not the arbitrary whims of a foppish rake, as many would have us believe. On the contrary, they were a breeding strategy which emphasised an individual's fitness as a lover or a husband capable of siring offspring and demonstrated his ability to pay for their upbringing. Thus, such fashions could be said to have been dictated by the deepest unconscious desires of members of the female sex who instinctively look for what Prudence Glynn in *Skin to Skin* (1982) terms: "the territorial prerogative" — the offer of a safe and well-provided-for nest.

REVOLUTIONARY TIMES

The French Revolution put a dramatic end to such display. When the proletariat came to power in 1789, male fashions throughout mainland Europe and even, to some extent, in England and America, changed radically and rapidly. The proletariat's hatred of the nobility, excessive wealth and privilege, was so great that any sign of opulence in dress aroused their fury. As a means of self-defence the fashionable men of the day discarded their elaborate and costly modes and accepted that, as an expediency, they should wear the simple dress of the people.

Initially the Revolution wiped out class distinction throughout Europe. Vast fortunes had been lost as a result of the dramatic social changes and it was impossible for many of those who had survived to continue their lives of ease and luxury. It therefore became imperative for them to enter the world of commerce and with this changed status came a changed outlook on life, resulting in a permanent change in clothing styles.

As manufacturing industries prospered during the 19th century and trade between the European countries boomed, the leaders of the wealthy middle class became the fashion leaders of the western world. Being prudent men, their clothes reflected their prudent and often puritanical attitudes. Gone were the elaborate wigs, the powder, the paint, the brightly-coloured velvet coats, the embroidered waistcoats and the voluminous silk pantaloons.

In the realms of men's finery, however, traditions die hard. Although the excesses of pre-Revolutionary days have never reappeared in their entirety, the wigs, the lace ruffs, the silk knee breeches, the velvet jackets and the great cloaks of office live on in the vestments worn by judges, barristers, lords and barons, university chancellors, members of the few remaining royal families, the clergy, lord mayors and various other high-ranking and privileged members of western society.

BEAU BRUMMELL

Professor Flugel referred to the unilateral decision by men to forego their right of sexual display, as *The Great Masculine Renunciation*. "Man," he said, "abandoned his claim to be considered beautiful. He henceforth aimed at being useful. So far as clothes remained of importance to him, his utmost endeavour could lie only in the direction of being *correctly* attired, not of being elegantly or elaborately attired." They adopted either the obviously commercial ideals, or the slightly more discreet styles advocated by George (Beau) Brummell so that a gentleman of leisure could distinguish himself from the less well-born by small details. It was important, of course, that these details were so discreet as not to be noticed by the average man — otherwise he might be tempted to copy them. But they should be of sufficient importance to be noticed by other gentleman and by women of society. This is why Beau Brummell became famous for his obsession with putting on a cravat. He refused to wear jewellery except for a cravat-pin of diminutive size, a modest signet-ring, and a prosaic watch-chain: these, he advocated, were as far as a gentleman should go in terms of expensive decoration.

Brummell also decreed that a gentleman should no longer wear his ducal riband and garter to proclaim his aristocratic lineage. Instead, he should dress anonymously in a plain suit which had been immaculately cut, fitted and made by the very best hand tailors of London's Savile Row. Such a suit entailed many days of arduous work, with skilled craftsmen being involved in every stage of its making, so that the elite would be able to notice each discreet point which had involved many hours of extra labour. And of course Brummell insisted that only the most experienced tailors should work on his suits, demanding that the best cutter, best fitter, best collar maker, best liner, best trouser maker, best pocket maker, best seamer and the best stay-stitcher be reserved for his orders and those of his friends.

▲ Fashionable city wear for gentlemen in the 1820s was the top hat and tails, based on the hunting suit of the English landed gentry

▲ Traditional styles of male dress of the pre-Revolutionary period live on in the vestments of the church and the ceremonial robes of high office

Changes in fashion correspond with a hidden network of forces that operate on society — political, economic, and psychological factors all play their part.
Cecil Beaton 1954

▲ ▶ *During the early years of the 19th century, Napoleon established a style of dress that made people forget about his lack of height because his clothes were so distinctive, and the very outfit has conjured up the image of the little Emperor ever since. Beau Brummell was greatly influenced by Napoleon's mode of dress and he combined it with the attire of the British landed gentry to create the forerunner of today's threepiece suit*

The difference between a gentleman's suit and an ordinary suit should be so subtle that only a gentleman could notice it.
Beau Brummell

LE LION

He was also a fanatic over cleanliness. History rightfully credits Brummell with making English gentlemen clean for the first time — a feat even the Puritans had failed to accomplish. He changed his linen at least three times a day. He had the soles of his shoes polished as meticulously as the uppers. He had three barbers to cut his hair — one to attend to the front, another to the back, and the third to the sides. He had four skilled craftsmen to make his gloves, one of whom was such an expert in the making of the thumb that the thumbnail had to be specially trimmed before he put on a new pair. Brummell was, as Pearl Binder points out in *The Peacocks Tail* (1958), "a modern man. Hollywood is where he really belongs. Nobody knew the news-value of his affectations better than he did, and the legend he was so skilled in creating has lasted successfully into our own times. He could always think up something new. He told infatuated young noblemen that his recipe for boot varnish was to add champagne. He let it be widely known that he made his valet wear all his new clothes first as they came from the tailors, so that they should not look too vulgarly new when he wore them himself."

When Beau Brummell was told of a man who was so well dressed in the smartest new fashions that everybody turned round to look at him, Brummell replied 'Then he was not well-dressed. The world is silly to admire such absurdities.'
Mens Tailoring 1934

we couldn't look better.

TOP MAN
You couldn't look better.

▲ ▲ *The lounge suit, so called because the originators of this style lived off handsome private incomes and did not have to work, has changed little over the past hundred years*

Brummell was no accident. He had to happen, and to happen just then, as he was formed by the social changes then taking place. And he was copied, not because he had great style, but because he came to symbolize the new age, the power of shopkeepers, of merchants and manufacturers. His mode of dress was exactly right for the social climate of his epoch. Brummell was in fact a self-made man, a man of very humble origins, a man on the make who is believed to have started life as a valet, and who was both shrewd and intelligent: a man who over the intervening years has come to symbolize the new attitude to male dress.

Some historians regard the 19th century *Brummell Style* as

▲ ▲ ▲ *Details in the styling of the ubiquitous lounge suit have been influenced by the young dandies of every era*

"the valets' revenge on society. Valeting it into a cleanliness bordering on mania and at the same time taking all the gaiety and pleasure out of male dress."

THE RISE AND FALL OF THE TAILORED SUIT

In the early 19th century, the thriving middle-class males were soon joined in their boardrooms by many of the surviving aristocrats, many of whom had lost their fortunes during the social upheavals and now had to work for a living. These aristocrats wished, once again, to visibly establish their lineage (as this added to their employability) without returning to their previous extravagances. They achieved this by wearing a style adapted from the sporting field. It was no ordinary sport they chose, but the high-status and undeniably elite pastime of the leisured classes: hunting.

And so it was that an adaptation of the tailored clothes originally worn for horse-riding became normal day wear. The male hunting jacket — cut away at the front so it would not bulge over the saddle and with tails at the back, worn with straight trousers adapted from the proletarian style, became synonymous with good breeding. And so did the stiff top hat, originally worn only when out hunting as a sort of early crash-helmet. By the mid-19th century, top hat and tails had become the standard wear throughout the upper strata of commerce and banking, even by those who had never ridden a horse.

With the passage of time, this mode gradually lost its high status as an increasing number of people began to wear it, and the landed gentry had to turn to a new area of sporting activity. This time it was the turn of shooting and fishing: both costly, leisured pursuits which were only possible if you owned vast tracts of land with your own rivers and moors. Again the original designs were slightly modified to make them suitable for everyday wear. Tough tweeds became check lounge suits; the traditional shooting hat became the original bowler; the softer fishing hat, a trilby.

As the lounge suit was adopted by a new generation of socially-acceptable young men, they abandoned the original checks and opted for more sombre colours and cut. The tailcoat was by now *passé* for all daytime social events and, as *morning dress*, retreated to the formalized context of weddings and other ceremonial events. The *evening dress* version became the form of garb now only worn by head waiters at expensive restaurants. In its place came the ubiquitous dinner jacket, the newly-formalized, black-or-white version of the lounge suit.

The famous mistress of Louis XV, Madame de Pompadour, understood the necessity to distinguish herself from her rivals so that she would clearly be seen as being the number one female in the court of Versailles. This she did by inventing a style of dressing that required the skills of the best Paris dressmakers and projected all the requisite symbols of wealth and power and yet recalled the freshness and simplicity of the shepherdess and the rosy-cheeked milkmaid

No sooner had the lounge suit reached the hallowed status of everyday wear, than it became necessary for those of social standing to replace it with some new form of expensive sportswear. The answer was the hacking jacket which was originally worn with plus-fours. This was quickly followed by the yachting blazer with its shiny brass buttons, worn with flannel trousers. But in more recent years most men of wealth and social standing have opted to wear the hand-tailored Savile

A CORRECT VIEW OF THE NEW MACHINE FOR WINDING UP THE LADIES

Row suit with its appeal resting not so much on style, but on a Beau Brummell approach to detail. Of course, men still wished to signal to women their desireablity as a lover as well as a provider. Now they had to find more subtle ways than the padded nether-hosen and tightly-fitting *braquette*. They relied instead upon socially-accepted forms of symbolism such as the 7½ inch/19 cm long, 1½ inch/4 cm wide top-stitched fly; the last vestige of the cod-piece which acted as a perfectly placed penis echo.

It is hardly surprising therefore, as Terence Dixon and Martin Lucas so rightly point out in *The Human Race* (1982): "that a substantial element of male sexual signalling through clothing should emphasise wealth, position, power, and high status generally. In the developed world today, this mostly means the conventional suit and tie, or something very similar." However they also noted that new variations are beginning to occur, particularly where some males consider themselves of such high status that they hardly need to display this with their clothes. Such people may wear casual clothes with an extremely expensive pair of shoes, a costly wrist watch, or a superb car (a symbol of which is displayed on their key ring) which says, "I have such high status that I don't need to wear regulation clothes to prove it. But just in case there is the slightest doubt, you have only to imagine what this exquisite little detail cost."

CORSETS AND CRINOLINES

"Clothes maketh the man" according to the old cliché, but as has been pointed out many times over the past few centuries, "clothes maketh the woman more so." Of course, like all clichés, they contain a strong element of truth.

▲ The great French beauty, Madame Récamier, was responsible for promoting the transparent Grecian style of dress that became popular after the French Revolution. In fact she demonstrated how far a naturally attractive and well-shaped women could rise in society without having recourse to ornate costumes and expensive jewels

▲ *When the Grecian mode was at its height, Madame Récamier's great rival, Madame Hannelin is reputed to have promenaded in the Tuileries Gardens in nothing more than a sheath of dampened gauze. This scanty fashion began to wane in France by 1803 under the influence of Napoleon who insisted upon a display of expensive finery in his court to help boost the flagging French economy. The Naked Fashion, as it had then become known, lingered on in England and in parts of North America until the early 1820s*

The greatest provocations of lust are from our apparel.
Robert Burton *Anatomy of Melancholy*

Women's dress has been influenced throughout history largely by the same motives that clothe men — the desire to signal sexual availability, to fuel sexual desire and to display wealth and power. But there is one very important difference between men and women's motives. While men, in general, dressed to please, excite and attract women; women were more often than not dressing to outdo one another.

SEXUAL INVITATION

Women have gone to great lengths to signal their sexual availability. In the early 1800s, for instance, there was a fashion in France for transparent, clinging dresses worn with no underclothing at all. Between the 14th and mid-17th centuries, the traditional laced-up opening down the front of bodices worn by all women who could afford to wear a fashionably-cut dress, rather than a sack-like covering, was referred to as "the gates of hell" and "common shop of temptation." And for a good reason. Unmarried women who wished to signal their nubility, virginity and availability for marriage would often leave their bodices loose and open or even entirely undone, exposing the whole of the breasts. As one commentator wrote of these nubile women in 1594: "their round roseate buds immodestly lay foorth, to shew at their hands there is fruit to be hoped." Another wrote that these young women often appeared "in Publick quite naked from the Top of the Head, almost to the Waist, displaying their Neck, Shoulders, Breasts, and parts of their Waists quite bare." In France and Spain this fashion was referred to as an "intolerable crime" and a "pernicious scandal" whilst in Italy and elsewhere it was generally accepted, and referred to as *Vespoitrinement à la Venise* with the more fashionable women of that city reportedly rouging their nipples.

The fashion for displaying women's breasts and nipples has changed over the years, but whether concealed or fully displayed these mammary glands have, in western society at least, never lost their sexual allure. As Havelock Ellis and many others have pointed out: "Among Europeans, the importance of this region is so highly esteemed that the general rule against the exposure of the body is in its favour abrogated." This has been amply borne out throughout western sartorial history.

LUSTFULNESS

Many moralists have concluded that women are at least three times more lustful than men. In 1621 Robert Burton wrote:

"of women's unnatural insatiable lust, what country, what village does not complain?" Many other contemporary commentators also remark on what appears to have been an insatiable sexual appetite at most of the European royal courts between the 15th and 18th centuries; the court at Versailles, the English court and the court of the Hapsburgs were particularly notorious.

▼ Much nonsense has been perpetrated about the steel chastity belt introduced in the Middle Ages. It was certainly not a case of the macho husband locking up his wife and galloping off to the Crusades with the key. The device was probably introduced by the women themselves as a form of teasing selection, the gift of the key being entirely at the wearer's discretion

Even the great Russian court of St Petersburg was famous for its sexual exploits and Fernando Henriques, writing of Catherine the Great, stated that: "her need for sexual satisfaction was inexhaustible. When she was 60 a young lieutenant in the horse-guards, Plato Zubof, by his charm and manner caught her eye. The machinery was set in motion. The young man of 25 was examined by the Empress's English physician, Mr Rogerson, and by Miss Protas, the royal *éprouveuse*. The latter's function apparently was to test out the sexual abilities of potential favourites. All was successful and Zubof was duly installed."

Gina Luria comments in *Everywoman* (1976) on Catherine's appointment of an *éprouveuse*: "Not even England under the Regent had such an office under the crown," and she goes on to say that Henriques had mentioned that the behaviour of Catherine "was not an isolated phenomenon. The majority of the ladies at court tried to emulate their sovereign by keeping men as favourites." As indeed had many other powerful women both before and since. The young men of the court dressed to attract attention by exaggerating their sexual attributes and the women presented their most alluring sexual features as attractively as possible. Fashionable display became very coquettish as well as extraordinarily expensive.

▲ Decorating pubic hair and rouging nipples was very popular during the 17th century

THE TREASURE CHEST

From time to time attempts were made to control these expensive displays, as various monarchs perceived the necessity of assigning limits to the escalating extravagance. In the mid-16th century, for instance, Henry IV of France issued an edict restricting external displays of wealth in the French court. In a very early edition of the *La Belle Assemblée* we read: "the fair sex, being restricted in the employment of exterior ornament, concentrated the science of the toilette and of dress by inventing a fashion which certainly no law could have touched because it was out of sight." And further research in this *court and fashionable magazine* reveals a report of the death of the Marchioness d'Estrées, who was killed in a sedition at Essowe toward the end of the 16th century: "It appears that her body was left in the streets very indecently exposed and furnished an opportunity of observing a fashion which had been for some time introduced among women of quality. It was not only the hair of the head that they adorned with crimp ribbon of different colours."

My research also reveals that the decorating of the body in the mode of the Marchioness d'Estrées was by no means new, nor was it confined to the use of different-coloured ribbons. In fact, one writer of the period states that fresh flowers were also used, as were many precious and semi-precious jewels that were neatly tied into position in a random pattern with the flowers. Some ladies used perfume that was discreetly located and they also plucked out the fringe areas of the pubic region, somewhat in the oriental manner, to achieve a more aesthetically decorative shape, whilst others preferred small plaits adorned with baroque pearl droplets — suggesting that such a fashion gave rise to the term "a woman's treasure chest" and "to obtain the favour of a lady" was an expression to be taken in a literal sense.

TOP OF THE HEAP DRESSING

Women of high social standing also displayed their wealth by wearing very tight and very high shoes, some with eight-inch/ 20 cm platforms, plus an extra five inches/12.5 cm at the heel which added 13 inches/32.5 cm to their height and required the assistance of two maids or footmen to be able to walk. Or they wore hip panniers which often projected 24 inches/ 80 cm on each side, giving them a width of over 5 feet/1.52m — which required extra space when standing, a full *chaise longue* when sitting, and a special coach or sedan-chair in order

▲ *The art of body decoration, revived here by the magazine* Club International *in the 1970s*

[Top] The Empire *style replaced the Naked Fashion in England in the 1820s. Breasts were still on display, but pushed up and out with the aid of lace-up corsets and padding*

to get from one place to the next. Very high and elaborate wigs were also worn to emphasise their superior social position as were neck ruffs of expensive lace supported on wire frames up to 26 inches/65 cm wide.

BACK TO SIMPLICITY

The French Revolution changed the rules overnight. In place of extravagance, simplicity reigned. The female dress of 1800 was but a simple layer of undecorated Indian muslin generally worn directly over the naked body, "draped in the *Grecian* style". It would seem that the proprietors of the new fashion magazines were of the opinion that both men and women would now be free from the extravagant tyranny of fashionable dress, although, of course, very few had actually been wealthy enough to afford such luxury and prior to the popular uprising of 1789 had dressed in a very plain and uninteresting style.

Another magazine editorial suggested that the new near-

▲ *Elizabeth I fully understood the importance of dressing for success as can be seen in this portrait* The Procession of the Queen to Blackfriars *by Marcus Gheeraerts*

▲ ▲ ▲ *The fashionable styles worn by the nouveau riche in the 19th century were promoted in the monthly fashion magazines, sparking off a demand for an ever-changing parade of new and elaborate styles, with the emphasis firmly on the price tag*

naked fashion was "like the sunshine introduced into the paintings of Titian. It animates the figure and gives them all the embellishment that is needed . . . displaying the true beauty of the person to the greatest possible advantage," and the article continues: "never were our fair females so sparsely dressed, covered with nothing more than transparent shawls, that float and flutter over their breasts, which are clearly seen through them; and with a robe so fine that the wearer seemed to be almost naked."

Many fashion historians who have commented on these post-revolutionary fashions thought that they were quite indecent and that they had certainly gone too far in trying to destroy social decorum. Oskar Fischel, in *Modes and Manners of the XIX Century* (1909) commented: In 1798, released from the rule of the *Terror*, the Parisian ladies, who had been forced to forbear the pleasures of a new mode since 1789, now carried the *Grecian* fashion to an extravagant excess; under the pretence of wishing to appear classic, the new mode was soon more correctly to be designated the *naked fashion*. Not only did corsets and under-petticoats disappear, but all other garments were also discarded . . . The more fashionable of these ladies strove as to which of them could put on the least clothing. No one spoke of anyone as being *well dressed*, but as *beautifully shaped*, and it became an amusement in society to weigh a lady's garments — her whole clothing, including shoes and ornament was not allowed in 1800 to weigh over eight ounces. And there were reports of ladies walking in the garden of the Tuileries clad only in a gauze veil." Elizabeth B Hurlock in her book published in 1929 concluded: "after The Revolution there was such a reaction in clothing that the period will go down in history as one of the most immoral in the annals of fashion. Licentiousness in dress was thus a fitting accompaniment to the licentiousness which characterized the manners of the time.

NOUVEAU RICHE

During the industrial expansion of the early 19th century and the breaking up of the aristocratic ways of life which had dominated western fashion for many hundreds of years, a new way of dressing quickly evolved which was based, not on social standing, but on newly-acquired wealth. We read in a copy of *La Belle Assemblée* from 1809 that: "the more wealthy classes of society are constantly devising new modes for marking the artificial distinction between themselves and those who are not so rich in worldly possessions, by a difference in dress . . ." A point developed later by Doris Langley Moore in *The Women in Fashion* (1949) in which she concluded that changing fashions were "a phenomenon based on forms of class distinction, [which] can operate only when the social order is fluid, when the structure of society is such that each stratum is able to take on the manner of life of another stratum which seems to have more advantages. The envied class wishes to maintain its separateness and tries to keep imitators at a distance by creating differences of dress which will establish the prestige of its members visibly and immediately . . ."

During the mid-19th century and again in the first two decades of this century, styles changed at a steady rate — designs worn one year being considered out-of-date the next. However during the periods of greatest wealth, such as the mid 1860s, fashionable styles changed even more rapidly; sometimes from month to month and occasionally from week to week. This, of course put great pressure on the inventors of the new modes and inevitably resulted in styles which could only be worn by those whose sole function in life was to be fashionable. The more extreme these fashions became, the more they tended to clearly and visibly display their wearer's *fashionability*. These modish outfits were generally so large and cumbersome that the woman would require the aid of at least one if not two maids when dressing and, once dressed, a special coach for transportation. All of which was clearly indicated to the observer.

EROGENOUS ZONES

Peter Fryer explains in his book *Mrs Grundy: Studies in English Prudery* (1963): "the changes in women's fashions are basically determined by the need to maintain men's sexual interest, and therefore to transfer the primary zone of erotic display once a given part of the body has been saturated with attractive power to the point of satiation." And he goes on to say that "each new fashion seeks to arouse interest in a new erogenous zone to replace the zone which, for the time being, is played out" — but, of course, without ever displaying the primary erogenous zone, except in one's most intimate moments.

TIGHT LACING

The prototype of the much-maligned laced-up corset was first used in Crete during Minoan times when young women are known to have laced in their waists during festive occasions

▲ Poets and social commentators praised the scanty Naked Fashion of the early 19th century on the grounds of its social equality

▲ In the west, we have built up an elaborate system of fashion changes which orchestrate the display of erogenous zones. One year it's the turn of the thighs, the next, the breast

Coquetry is the Mother of Modesty.
Groose *1897*

in order to enhance their appearance. Lacing-in of the waist was also practised in ancient Greece, and is referred to by both Homer and Herodotus, who also make reference to the practice of bust binding.

The laced-up corset was fashionable during Roman times, as was a form of shaped brassiere made to accentuate the curves of the breast, but these devices seem to have fallen out of favour during the rise of Christianity, and did not re-appear as items of fashionable wear in Europe until the 12th century on the return of the First Crusaders.

As more and more exotic Eastern items became available on the return of the Second and Third Crusades (the knights and many of the soldiers brought back vast amounts of plunder) along with the growth of mercantile wealth during the period of the Renaissance, the wives and daughters of the wealthy merchant classes gradually began wearing these laced-up corsets which, by the 14th century, were made of intricately-cut panels of leather and linen. Soon the families of the growing middle class also began wearing a modified version of the corset which they laced down the front (the original corset was laced up the back and required the assistance of a maid). The corset became an accepted mode of apparel, designed to pull in the waist and push up the breasts so as to display an ample amount of *embonpoint*.

By the early 17th century, women's sexual emphasis was firmly centred on the waist, which was made even narrower than ever before with the aid of steel and whalebone corsets, and the invention of a lacing aid which, it was said, "could winch inches off a healthy woman." A narrow waist was a clear statement that a woman was not pregnant, which acted as a challenge to the virility of most men. It made her bustline higher and more pronounced, her hips more curvaceous, but more importantly it made the visual statement that the wearer was unable to work — in fact she was often unable to move about without the aid of a maid and a footman — clearly and unequivocally declaring a position of social superiority and great wealth which in turn added to her sex appeal, many men finding great wealth and a superior social position sexually exciting.

Havelock Ellis discusses the steel and whalebone corset at great length. As Ellis says: "not only does the corset render the breasts more prominent", by pushing them upwards and making them appear even larger in contrast to the narrowed waist, but "it has the further effect of displacing the breathing

▲ ▲ ▲ Visible erogenous zones shift across cultures and across time. In Japan, the nape of the neck has always been regarded as extremely sexy, and in Europe, with the advent of mini skirts and hot pants, the thighs came into their own. Men's fashions are also subject to the vagaries of what is and isn't acceptable. In the 1930s girdles were advertised which completely concealed the distinctive male crotch bulge

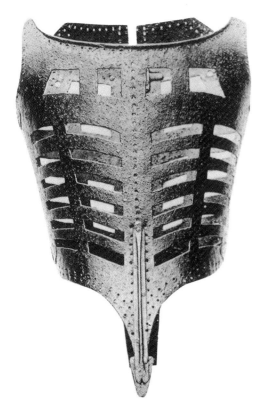

◀ ▲ ▲ The corset has taken on many guises over the years. It seems to have started in Crete with the Minoans (above left). In medieval times many aristocrats wore corsets of steel inlaid with gold and precious stones (left). At other times the corset has often an appearance as an integral part of the dress as shown above in a fashion illustration from the late 19th century

The corset must be regarded as the chief instrument of sexual allurement which the armoury of costume supplies to a woman, for it furnishes her with a method of heightening at once her two chief sexual secondary characteristics, the bosom above, and the hips and buttocks below.

Havelock Ellis *1905*

activity of the lungs in an upward direction. The advantage from the point of sexual allurement thus gained being that additional attention is drawn to the bosom from the respiratory movement imparted to it . . ."

The compression of the waist by means of the corset has had criticism over the centuries, but none more forceful than that which was published in the *English Ladies' Newspaper* in 1874: "We deem the Chinese cruel who bandage the feet of the girl babies, so that the grown woman have only stumps upon which they can feebly totter; we think that the flat-headed Indian mother evidences her folly when she straps the head of her infant into what she considers a better form than nature has given it. But the women of our own country who have endeavoured by artificial means since childhood to produce an unnatural slenderness of waist are more barbarous and foolish by far than either of these. It seems impossible, that in this enlightened age, there exists women who still follow the barbarous custom of tight-lacing for themselves and their children. Long tight bodies may be fashionable, but tight-lacing is both a folly and a crime."

POOR LITTLE ME!

In recent years, many historians and others have tried to put the blame for the use of the corset on to the men of the period. But this is to refute the mass of evidence to the contrary. Many husbands, lovers and physicians have gone on record as opposing the wearing of tightly-laced corsets for women (although many of the men were wearing them themselves, as this was the male fashion of the time). Many religious leaders also spoke out against the use of corsets by women — not however because of the physical dangers involved but because corsets "raised the lust of men" and they allowed women to display more easily "that which God himself had ordained should be kept covered."

▲ The starlet at the centre of attention here is revealing far less than she would in a bikini, but the excitement comes not from the degree of nudity but from the powerful symbolism of the corset and all its trimmings

◀ Many people believe that it was the male who, over the years, forced the female into a variety of constricting or ungainly garments so that she would be incapable of surviving life's daily traumas without his manly assistance. But it is much more likely that such styles were invented by women in order to keep the male in a state of constant attention to their self-imposed helplessness

▶ All new fashions tend to send a shudder through the spine of those in authority, as changing fashions are a visible reminder that there are still aspects of everyday life beyond the control of the politician or the pulpit. But the fact is that the very condemnation of a fashion adds considerably to its attractiveness. The ecclesiastics of the 18th and 19th centuries seemed oblivious to the counter-productive nature of their criticisms as people vied with one another to be seen wearing to advantage that which had been most vehemently condemned

One must forgive fashion everything; it dies so young.
Jean Cocteau

▲ Over the centuries women have employed a whole array of pads, cushions, bolsters and wire cages to change the shape of their hips and buttocks. The example above dates from the 16th century

◀ Venetian courtesans of the 1590s wore distinctive breeches as a mark of their profession and their chopines, which added up to 20 inches/50 cms to their height, rendered them incapable of walking unaided

However, as many writers have pointed out: "most women do not choose their mode of dress to please men, but merely to raise their ardour." Nor do they wear new fashions to please the ecclesiastics. In fact if the fashionable styles worn by women were primarily intended to please men they would have been better advised to avoid wearing all extremes in dress — including those styles requiring a tightly-laced corset, bum-rolls or panniers. In fact, these, and similar constricting styles, seem to have been worn to keep male admirers in a state of constant attention to a woman's self-imposed helplessness, to raise her own body awareness and to annoy other women by coping more successfully with a difficult style and managing to appear more attractive within it. As Professor Flugel perspicaciously put it: "Man is so irresistibly attracted to woman that he will love her even in the most outrageous and hideous contractions not, however, because of them, but in spite of them."

'BUMMES LIKE A BARRELL'

Women have used padding to increase the size of their breasts and their buttocks since the days of the Ancient Greeks. In the 16th century many women wore a hip bolster as an alternative to the farthingale — the farthingale being a series of wooden hoops suspended from the waist to hold the skirt out from the body and give it a conical shape — whilst the hip bolster was a padded sausage-shaped cushion held out with hoops of whalebone to emphasize the *derrière*. This hip bolster quickly became known as the 'bum-roll', making the "buttokes brode" and giving women "a bumme like a barrell wyth whoopes at the skyrte, [which] swelled out the skyrte to make the buttocks most monstrously rounde." It was a fashion that was destined to re-appear several times during the next 300 years, and which reached its most exaggerated form in the 1870s in the shape of a large wire contraption known as the bustle, constructed to hold out up to ten metres of fabric.

The bustle had followed on from another wire contraption known as the crinoline which was fashionable during the late 1850s and 1860s and in concept was much the same as the farthingale. Instead of wooden hoops that measured up to 3 feet/1 metre across, the crinoline was made of wire hoops suspended from the waist by tapes. The contraption often measured 7 to 8 yards/7.5 metres around the hem.

The crinoline and bustle styles , both worn with tightly-laced corsets to emphasize the narrowness of the waist, must

▲ ▲ ▲ Improving on nature. A rounded posterior has been a much sought-after attribute. It could be achieved by tight lacing of the waist and abundantly ruffled drawers (the French actress, Polaire, is pictured centre displaying her 15 inch/37 cm wasp waist) or by the addition of false, padded curves

Well-shaped buttocks are a distinctive feminine feature much admired everywhere, especially among black races. These young black athletes have retained their rounded buttocks even when devoid of all excess fat

have made the wearers very conscious of their bodies. The wide skirts displayed to advantage the characteristic female carriage by highlighting the vibratory movement which is naturally produced by the way a female walks. The heightening of body awareness also tended to persuade the wearers that their clothes were extensions of themselves and that admiration for the dress was, in fact, admiration for the person within.

This may be one of the reasons why the desire to display "bummes like a barrell" did not disappear with the demise of the bustle, and adaptions of the bum-roll re-appeared in modified form in the 1900s and again briefly in the late 1930s and mid-1940s.

THE FACE

In a series of articles on *The Propensity of the Female Sex for Dress* in an early 19th century edition of *Ackermann's Repository of Arts*, we read that since earliest times it has been agreed "that whatever makes a woman more beautiful, whatever sets off their charms and the gifts they have received from nature, is their legitimate right." And the writer continues: "if a young woman has little more than a beautiful face and fine complexion with which to attract the attention of members of the opposite sex, then her mode of dress must be used to the greatest possible

▲ ▼ *Hats and headdresses have, until recently, been an important part of a woman's sexual armoury. They add height, which adds to the wearer's importance, and they exaggerate the movements of the head, which draws attention to the wearer and concentrates the observer's interest on her eyes, nose, cheeks and lips, all of which are very sexual in nature*

▶ The human face is a remarkable signaller of sexual arousal: lips redden, eyes sparkle, cheeks and earlobes blush. It comes as no surprise that the female face has become a major attractant for the opposite sex

▲ ▲ Various means of drawing attention to the face have included the wearing of beauty patches, great neck ruffs and frills that completely surround the face

advantage . . . Dress is but a frame for the face, and by embellishing the body it draws attention to the eyes, the cheeks, the mouth, the hair. And when a young woman smiles, desire is immediately excited, and the glint of her eyes awakens an involuntary passion."

Many writers have commented upon the western obsession with the face over all other erogenous zones. This would appear to advantage only those who are naturally endowed with fine facial features. Most of these writers believe however that the face owes its exalted position to "the progressively widening irradiation of the sexual feeling during the various states of arousal through the features of the face." In more recent times, Desmond Morris has elaborated on this fact by drawing our attention to the physiological changes that occur during sexual excitement: the lips swell and become redder, the cheeks blush, the eyes glisten and the soft areas around the eyes become vibrant. In fact the face, during our evolution has become the most animated of all of our erogenous zones. It is of little wonder then, that our Caucasian ancestors chose this particular characteristic to emphasize, particularly as these changes are much more pronounced in the white races owing to the normal paleness of our skin.

By the use of cosmetics, beauty aids and various forms of dress our female forebears learnt to control changes to the facial features. They also fully understood that the naked body gives testimony only to nature's gifts which are intended to excite the male for the purpose of the sexual act itself, and not to keep members of the opposite sex in a constant state of anticipation. Thus, through an elaborately contrived ritual of reticence, concealment, restraint and modesty, women have gradually transferred the interest of the opposite sex to the face, and to other areas of erogenous display only as they choose.

▲ Fancy dress has been used as a way of introducing new ideas into
everyday fashion, as well as scoring points over one's peers

▲ Turn-of-the-century styles left only the
hands and the face exposed to view

ONE-UPMANSHIP

On closer examination of the objections raised to women's
fashions between the Middle Ages and the beginning of the
present century, one is forced to conclude that moral
condemnation and religious criticism often increased the
desirability of these modes. Robert Burton pointed out in 1621:
"women are of such a disposition, they will mostly covet that
which others have attempted to deny them." And other writers
have also theorized on this very point, with more than one
stating that: "women of fashion simply vie with each other
to see who can stand out most effectively from the group,
in those very garments that have been condemned."

It has been noted by many writers that humans tend to
act differently according to the way they are dressed, taking
on a more or less superior status according to the style of
garments and accessories they are wearing. This can be clearly
seen when actors and actresses wear costume to help them
portray certain characters. And my research shows that
although fashionable women throughout history have been

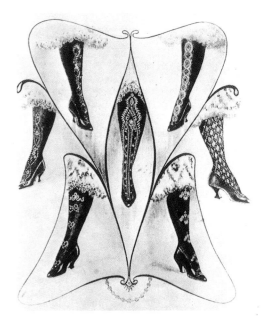

▲ Adventurous women of fashion took to
wearing high-heeled shoes with low-cut
vamps and embroidered stockings which, if
glimpsed by the opposite sex, would draw
attention to their ankles (how shocking!) and
put the gentlemen in mind of what lay above

fully aware that their extravagant garments tended to heighten their sex appeal, the real motive for wearing such styles appears to be one of vying with the members of their own sex. A battle within the sexes rather than one of attraction between them.

The admiration such styles created amongst their peers enhanced their self esteem which in turn enhanced their social position — a social position which to them was of the utmost importance. They achieved this by a continual display of frills, flounces, baubles, fringes, fine silks, metal cages, cane extensions, wigs, shoes and of course a wide range of facial aids and beautifiers that enabled them to retain their place at the centre of social, as well as sexual, attention. A place they have continued to hold until the present day.

FASHION MIRRORS LIFE

Despite what our parents and grandparents may say on the subject, and despite the fact that they have photographs to show how demure and dignified they were, the new fashionable styles worn by the majority of urban dwellers in their day were just as sexually provocative and shocking to their parents' generation as those being worn by the young avant-garde city dwellers of today. Of course, they are different in both concept and detail, as they represent the ideas and ideals of a totally different era. Fashionable styles of clothing are simply a product of their time.

But it wasn't only the clothing styles which were different. The social and economic situations were different, as was the popular music they listened to, the books they read, the kind of entertainments they enjoyed, the work they did, what they talked about, the food they ate, who they voted for, where they lived and many other aspects of everyday life.

COQUETTES AND COURTESANS

At the turn of the century, the love of opulence and decorative detail which had dominated all new fashionable styles since the mid-19th century was still at its height.

The *demi-mondaines* — the coquettes and courtesans — had risen to power during the Second Empire under the patronage of Napoleon III. They had such style that they gained enormous power and succeeded in totally removing the stigma of prostitution from their profession. Such was their exulted position in fashionable society towards the end of the 19th century that they exerted great influence over the princes, aristocrats, industrial barons and millionaires who openly

▲ Lily Langtry, known as the Jersey Lily, created a fashion for a new fabric, jersey, and pioneered a more fluid style of dress

▲ In the 19th century, the demi-mondaines flourished. They were attractive, intelligent women who were determined to climb the ladder to fame and fortune. They were the fashion leaders of the time and many a 'respectable' woman would follow where they led

competed for their favours. And the most famous of these *demi-mondaines* aroused great interest amongst the general public who avidly followed their amorous affairs and copied their fashionable styles. These ladies developed a prestige and a following similar to film stars in the golden age of Hollywood.

OFF WITH THE CORSETS!

By the end of the first decade of the 20th century, as society began to change in response to the changing times, a new style of fashion began to emerge which was more in tune with the new century. Spearheaded by two young French designers, Madeleine Vionnet and Paul Poiret, the obligatory corset was at long last abandoned and a new fluid dress style was introduced. Needless to say it was condemned as being "obscene" as well as "vulgar, wicked and ugly" by both the popular press and the clergy. This diatribe assured success, giving the new fashions a sort of magic allure with just the hint of exotic sexuality and sinfulness, which was precisely what the women of fashion wanted.

▲ American heiresses were competing with the stylish demi-mondaines and actresses for an aristocratic husband. Distinctive American female attributes — tall, broad-shoulders, fresh complexion, long legs and a love of sport — were soon destined to change the evolutionary path of 20th century fashion

▲▶ In 1908 the revolutionary young French couturier Paul Poiret published an album of designs reminiscent of the Grecian style worn by women of fashion in the early 19th century. Established society was outraged but it was exactly what the younger women wanted to distinguish themselves from the ageing, corseted and bejewelled demi-mondaines

▲ In June 1910 the first performance of
Diaghilev's ballet Schéhérazade was given in
Paris featuring Ida Rubenstein and Vaslav
Nijinsky who danced near naked in costumes
by Bakst. It was the catalyst that finally broke
all cultural ties with the Belle Epoque and
launched fashion in an entirely new direction

Later, when describing these new fashions, Poiret wrote that he had wearied of the heavy-breasted matrons, dowagers and the older *demi-mondaines*, and that he now favoured the Botticelli-style breasts of the younger women of fashion: "I favour small breasts that rise forth from the bodice like an enchanting testimonial to youth. Can anything be more captivating than this beauteous roundness? It is unthinkable that the breasts should be sealed up in solitary confinement in a castle fortress like the corset." And in a *Vogue* editorial on these new styles he is quoted as saying: "To dress a woman is not to cover her with ornaments; it is to underscore the endowments of her body, to bring them out and stress them. It is what a woman leaves off, not what she puts on, that gives her cachet." These were the ideas and ideals Poiret shared with Vionnet. And these were the ideas and ideals which were to dominate fashion for the next 50 years.

BALLETS RUSSES

Enormous changes were also taking place in the world of the arts, and in particular in ballet. The arrival in Paris of the *Ballets Russes*, headed by the Russian entrepreneur Sergei Diaghilev, turned the fashionable world on its ear. Their

▲ ▼ *After World War I life changed completely. Cars were everywhere, air travel had been introduced and jazz music had arrived. There was also a noticeable shortage of eligible young men, and the young women began to dress in sexually explicit clothing in order to attract a mate or a paramour. Beadwork that echoed the female genitals and see-through tops became almost commonplace*

performances were electrifying. Extravagant and sensual productions told frenzied tales of harem jealousies and intrigues, there were wild orgy scenes with near nude dancers, oriental splendour and undeniably barbaric costumes and scenery. The *Ballets Russes* acted as a catalyst in popularising the new mood and the new fashionable styles of the time, finally and irrevocably breaking all ties with the 19th century.

MIDDLE CLASS MADNESS

Freed from the middle class repression inherited from the 19th century the new younger generation eagerly embraced the new rebellious styles. The old and staid watched with increasing horror as they saw young *respectable* women painting their faces and throwing off their corsets and superfluous layers of clothing. Even more horrifying, these women were demanding the right to vote, to drive a car, to smoke in public, to dance the tango and to partake in active sports wearing clothes that revealed their legs. With the outbreak of the First World War in August 1914, some even demanded to join the army and work in munition factories. And it was during that war that dragged on for four years and three months, that ordinary women at last won the right to dress as they pleased in a style which suited them — free from constricting middle class ideals and outdated bigotry.

THE AFTERMATH OF WAR

The 1920s started within a few months of the official signing of the Versailles Peace Treaty. Millions of people had died and there was a noticeable shortage of young eligible males

▲ *In the mid 1920s, in an atmosphere of great change, it became fashionable to smoke Eastern drugs and to wear Eastern pyjamas*

◀▲ *As the 1920s progressed, dresses grew shorter. In 1925 the Archbishop of Naples declared that the death and devastation caused by an earthquake at Amalfi, "was due to the anger of God protesting against the present immodesty of dress." In Ohio a bill was introduced to prohibit any female over 14 "from wearing a skirt which does not reach that part of the foot known as the instep"*

throughout Europe. Young women had undertaken a great deal of manual work during the war. They had lived through their late teens and early 20s without the companionship of young men. Many had formed permanent relationships with other women, and many more had developed and learnt to maintain an independent way of life.

Others had discarded the sexual livery of modesty as, with a shortage of eligible young men, modesty had become decidedly outmoded, inconvenient and time-wasting. Many women yearned to exhibit their natural charms and sexual allure by divesting themselves of all but the scantiest of clothing. This is a natural reaction to disaster on a huge scale. The same thing happened in the Middle Ages after the Black Death wiped out one-third of Europe's population. There was a similar reaction in Rome after the Punic Wars, and in Germany after the Thirty Years' War when the number of eligible men had been reduced dramatically and female fashions became quite immodest. After the French Revolution, in which many more males perished than females, there was such a reaction in

clothing that the period has gone down in history as one of the most licentious in the annals of fashion.

Another factor for change was that many young girls had moved to the cities during the war to look for work. They had come from small communities where everyone knew everyone else's affairs and fashion changes had relatively little importance. In large communities, where there is an ever-changing population and single women have to draw attention to themselves in order to attract a companion, fashion plays a more important role and its influence is far greater.

FLOORING THE COMPETITION

In this atmosphere of great social change *competitive imitation* and *competitive display* became the driving forces of the new fashions, reaching the height of immodesty in the mid-1920s when it became almost obligatory for women to wear semi-transparent shifts which were cut low in the front and very short. Individuality was expressed in the choice of beadwork which was often very complex and was certainly very costly. Fashionable women wore high-heeled shoes with low-cut vamps to draw attention to their ankles and legs, and sheer stockings were worn to make the legs appear smooth and sexually attractive. The women who could afford the extra expense also wore silk lingerie with inset buttoned gussets, roulette trimmings and fine lace edging.

Cosmetics had also become very important in the 1920s, much to the disgust of the older generation who still associated their use with harlots and scarlet women. But under the influence of the Hollywood stars and beauty magazines, the young woman of the mid-1920s knew that cosmetics, special lotions and shampoos enabled her to make the most of her lips, her cheeks, her eyes and her hair. And this young woman soon learnt that the more attractive she made herself, the better chance she had for improving her work prospects, and for attracting a suitable companion.

THE HAVES AND HAVE-NOTS

At the end of the 20s the finances of the western world collapsed, triggered by the Wall Street Crash of October 1929. The resulting financial crisis created the Great Depression; many millions of people lost their jobs and they remained out of work throughout the early 30s. Strange as it may seem, this very lack of money created a new style of fashionable dress which was long and slender and expensive for those who were

▲ ▲ *Both European and American fashion became much sexier as censorship of the arts was gradually relaxed*

▲ *Hollywood glamour and luxury personified — Carole Lombard wearing a dress cut on the cross in the style of the couturier Madeleine Vionnet*

▲ *Busby Berkeley's camera celebrated the image of the leggy American chorus girl, and had a dramatic effect on popular fashion*

▼▼ *Throughout the 30s it was the film stars of Hollywood who were most admired for their glamour and sex appeal, and it was their suave or sexy styles that by the mid 30s most people aspired to*

lucky enough to afford such luxury items at a time of poverty.

The new dresses, when made by the really top couturiers of the period like Madeleine Vionnet — who incidentally had started her career designing the opulent lingerie of the *demi-mondaines* in the late 1890s — fitted like a second skin, showing the wearer's figure to perfection. They showed every ripple of the body, the curves of the natural bust line and the curves of the natural *derrière*. No corset or brassiere could be worn, nor could any other form of underclothing as the outline would have been clearly seen through the dress. They also showed the natural curves of the thigh, the slight indentation of the navel, the size and exact position of the erect nipple and many other curves and indentations which testified to the well-kept figure of those women who were wealthy enough to afford the best, or who had access to such wealth.

ANYTHING YOU SAY, MR DE MILLE

During World War I the film industry proliferated as people flocked to the cinemas to see the latest war news and to relax after a hard day's work in the munitions factories. By the early 1920s a weekly visit to the cinema had become an established routine. The star system had become well-established. The luxurious and daring clothes worn by stars

▲ ▲ *Images of fashion: above the ultimate glamour fashion photograph and on the left the idealised Hollywood image. Neither image bears much resemblance to reality, but both appeal strongly to the aspirations of the onlooker*

such as Lillian and Dorothy Gish, Gloria Swanson, Pearl White, Theda Bara, Marion Davies, Pola Negri, Mary Pickford and Clara Bow were an essential part of their allure. Everything about these stars' wardrobes was larger than life. Their diamonds were bigger, their furs were thicker, the silks they wore were softer and more clinging, and the chiffons were always more diaphanous.

Disrobing these film stars had become one of the film-makers' most absorbing preoccupations, especially for directors like Cecil B De Mille who invariably managed to twist the script in order to show a major star undressing for a sumptuous bath. De Mille realized that every item his stars wore had to be worth seeing, so he insisted that their shoes, stockings, lingerie, dresses, and wraps were all specially designed to make

You'd be surprised how tits figure in a girls career.
Louis B Mayer *1937*

▲ As World War II dragged on, British fashion magazines were obliged to promote the government's Utility clothing styles, which were based on outdated styles of the 1930s

◀ In the 1930s, topless bathing had been actively promoted in the magazines of the period. This drawing by Lepape was featured on the cover of French Vogue in 1934

▼ The laced-up corset enjoyed a renaissance in the late 1930s to help those whose natural curves and contours didn't quite match up to the feminine ideal

the most of each scene. He even sent to Paris for the famous designer Paul Iribe to design Gloria Swanson's dresses for his film *Male and Female* which are regarded as "among the most seductive and opulent costumes ever seen in a Hollywood film".

Mr De Mille, like many of the other leading directors of the period, was not so much concerned with being truly fashionable, as with being sensational and provocative. He knew that the fashions his movie stars wore would heighten the movie public's imagination, and that their imagination was very lurid indeed. He also knew that they yearned to see the exotic and the unusual, but above all else they yearned for glamour, glamour and more glamour.

THE GLAMOROUS MYTH

Soon the word glamour became synonymous with film fashions, and women everywhere sought to be as glamorous as their favourite stars. But the myth of glamour was perfection. Its disciples believed they could overcome their physical faults with cosmetics and beautiful dresses. What the public didn't realize was that their favourite star had spent many hours making-up, having her hair fixed, being sewn into a specially fitted dress and being photographed with a special camera under controlled lighting, with the negative being retouched before printing. In fact the film star photographs they so admired had nothing to do with real life.

Women were asked: "Do you like the thought of yourself with a tiny waist? Are you interested in the idea of having softly curved hips and a high rounded bust? Of course you are. Well these can be yours, with no more trouble than it takes to visit your local massage parlour." The sale of beauty creams increased dramatically when women were reminded that: "Now-a-days 25 is not *too* old, but it is half-way to 50, so 25 is not *too* young, either. So start taking care of your complexion. Save yourself from the ravages of time by using our new range of beauty products". Cosmetics soon became the equivalent of the Fairy Godmother's Wand. Women were told these potions could make an ugly duckling into a swan, and a homely maid into a beautiful woman.

REVELLING IN FEMININITY

In 1936 fashion leaders decreed a new style of décolletage which once again exposed the full swelling of the upper areas of the breasts with the exposed area discreetly stopping just above the nipples. Jewellery also flashed its costly message and there

▲▲ During the first years following the war, a new, skimpier sunbathing suit called the bikini made its appearance on Riviera beaches and soon spread throughout the world. In America they even invented a floating swimsuit, which allowed swimmers to strip in the water, swim alongside their bathing suit, and scramble back into it before emerging from the water

For the Garden : A Pinafore
Under a bright blue pinafore, a red and white
striped shirt. 2 guineas complete.

For Hard Work: Dungarees
Tight-ankled trousers and separate open-front
make rust dungarees practical; 2 guineas.

American 'Sailor Frock
A blue cotton sailor dress has white bra
iolate buttons, one breast pocket; 2 g

AMERICAN FASHIONS FOR SUMMER

ENGLISH women have always envied American summer clothes. In America, summer tub-frocks are so much cheaper, so much better cut than most of the sports and garden outfits made over here.
Just before the war, English shops started importing large quantities of gay, cheap fashions from the U.S.A. Now, of course, fashion imports are forbidden. So Picture Post has asked a London shop to make up a set of practical summer clothes copying American styles. American schemes, and American sizes. Here they are.
Big argument for these fashions is that you can them over and over again. Except for the two dresses, they are all made of cotton or linen that will in the wash-tub. They are all designed for hard wear, with pockets, without pleats.
Most of them have detachable aprons and bibs and se

▲ ▲ In America, cut off by the war from the fashion influence of Europe, they were going their own way, jiving and jitterbugging and showing off their long, shapely legs. But America's high fashion industry was losing confidence without the stimulation and inspiration of the French designers. They realised their homegrown designs lacked the joie de vivre that somehow seemed second nature to the French

were hints that a fur coat of lynx or sable "should be worn like a trophy, as in days of old when such furs were the gifts of kings to the ladies of their choice." And three years later in the spring of 1939, just a few months before the outbreak of Word War II, Paris announced that women would be "revelling in femininity once again — utterly, absolutely, and completely — in fashions which will make the most of all those feminine charms which God has seen fit to endow women with, in their battle to dominate the men in their lives. Women will add at least an inch to their already absurdly high-heels, and she will wear frills and ruffles and lace, and sashes, and fichus and filmy tulles. Yes even hoops, pads and bustles to display her most feminine of features." But before most women could visit their dressmakers, the wartime years of austerity had arrived and they had to make-do-and-mend until the end of hostilities and abide by the clothing decrees issued by their governments as to what they may or may not wear.

DIOR'S 'NEW LOOK'

In the spring of 1945 feminine fashions were once again beginning to appear in the shops and just two years later Christian Dior launched his *New Look* which was an instant success with the rich and fashionable and was destined to revolutionize women's wardrobes.

Although these *New Look* fashions were not as blatantly sexual as the styles worn after World War I, they nevertheless drew the eye of the beholder over all of the most alluring feminine features and by the use of padding and corsets, women's breasts, waists and buttocks were once again the centre of fashionable focus. Dior was on a winning roll, each collection being declared more inspired than the last. Reporters applauded the re-introduction of the laced-up corset which added inches to the bust line and whittled the waist. They praised his use of the plunging décolletage and thought the glove-like fit of the narrower waists was divine. They cooed approvingly over the new bustle-like peplum he used to emphasize the *derrière* and they advised their readers to buy the new pantie-girdles which, by the use of built-in padding, would add inches to their buttocks. They adored his longer skirts which focused attention onto the slender ankles of the model and they drooled over the lace-edged petticoats which could be glimpsed when she turned. And they declared that it was a crime to be seen wearing a dress or coat fashioned in last season's style.

▲ ▲ ▲ On the 12th February 1947, the unknown French couturier, Christian Dior, opened the doors of his small salon in the Avenue Montaigne to the assembled buyers and journalists who had come to view the new spring collections. It was his first show, and it was a sensation. In the following weeks the world's newspapers were full of his now legendary New Look. It was extravagant and feminine and it created great resentment amongst the poor and the unemployed

AND FOR THE MEN – ANOTHER SUIT

By comparison to the frenetic activity in the changing fashions of women's clothing during the first half of the 20th century, menswear changed very little. Men were still expected to visibly project that they were reliable breadwinners and that meant a plain, almost uniform style of suit which was thought to be in keeping with the commercial and industrial ideals founded in the mid-19th century. As London had become the financial capital of the western world, it was the English-style suit, with its reliance upon unchanging hand tailoring and attention to small details, which dictated the styles worn by most men.

Another reason for the survival of the English suit was because it flattered the physically inactive male, yet the same

▲ ▲ ▲ *The formality of traditional menswear relaxed in the late 1920s under the influence of the Prince of Wales (centre), who was quite a casual dresser, and the Hollywood stars who favoured relaxed, sporty clothes. But Hollywood's influence was a touch pernicious as it persisted in dressing its eccentric character actors in unconventional clothing, thus reinforcing the popular belief that unconventional dressers were necessarily weird if not downright dangerous*

style tended to deform the labouring classes. As pointed out earlier in this book, the business suit derives from the riding gear worn by the landed gentry. These young aristocrats were relatively tall to their breadth, and the cut and fit of their riding suits accommodated their need for walking, riding and sitting — but not for lifting, hauling, carrying or digging. By the mid-19th century the suit had been adapted to the needs of the upper echelons of business management — and as each suit was hand-tailored the style was adjusted to flatter the physically inactive senior executives of industry and commerce. Cheaper mass-produced suits however, tend to deform the physical appearance of lower management and the working classes making them, as John Berger put it in 1979, "appear un-coordinated, bandy-legged, barrel-chested, low-arsed . . . coarse, clumsy and brute-like". Which of course meant that when a member of lower management, or the working class, was in his *best* clothes, he always looked his *worst* in comparison to his *betters*. Hence the reason why the upper echelons of society insist that a suit be worn at all business meetings and social functions.

ENTER JAMES DEAN

To some extent this rigid code began to bend in the mid-1930s when some younger men started to copy the casual clothing styles of their favourite Hollywood stars. More women had also started to wear various items of male apparel, so menswear began to lose its symbolic and erotic appeal. Gradually the strict adherence to the suit was relaxed slightly, and a few

▲ ▶ *The Zoot suit (right) was all the rage amongst young Americans due to be drafted. When they were demobbed, the same fashion-conscious youths chose to be issued with double-breasted suits three sizes too big*

> *What women admire in men is a social superiority; that is the promise of being able to support a family in comfort and even in affluence. This they must show in their clothes.*
>
> James Laver *1955*

new styles were added to men's wardrobes for sportswear and for wearing at weekends. But owing to the war, further evolution was prevented by government regulations which froze all changes to civilian clothing styles.

At the end of hostilities, when the wartime restrictions were over, menswear changed rapidly. Between 1946 and 1956 these new styles were described as portraying "nothing less than a rebellious mood which is undermining our western way of life". Soon Teddy Boys, Mods, Rockers and Skin Heads became headline news. The styles worn by Elvis Presley and James Dean were widely copied, as were the later styles worn by the Beatles and the Rolling Stones. But alongside these innovations, the traditional styles persisted and young women in their wisdom, while encouraging the casual look for their boyfriends, still tended to marry the men who projected an allegiance to wealth and social standing.

▶ *James Dean heralded the era of T-shirts, jeans and bomber jackets and a welcome blurring of class and wealth barriers*

Signs and Symbols

Body presentation techniques have traditionally been used to inform the observer of the sex, cultural origin and social status of the wearer. Through an elaborate system of coded signs and symbols, clothes and adornments are also used to highlight physical attributes, to signal sexual maturity and to arouse sexual interest.

In the western world this system of coded messages has evolved over many hundreds of years, but in order to understand the messages, we must first learn the language.

▶ Modesty is relative. If this young warrior from the Alto Xingu in the Mato Grosso region of Brazil were to be asked to cover his genitals, he would be very embarrassed. To some races, the act of covering up an area of the body only serves to draw attention to a feature that, when naked, passes unnoticed

▲ The traditional heart-shape, perfectly demonstrated in this delightful picture, has its origins deep in our subconscious. It has very little to do with the very un-heart-shaped organ that pumps blood around the body. Many forms of dress symbolism also originate deep within our subconscious and greatly influence our choice of clothing

HUMANS ARE DIFFERENT

During our long period of evolution, our progenitors used their bodies to communicate with each other and this greatly affected how our bodies developed, with many features like our bare skin, upright posture and our distinctive facial features developing as an outward sign of our humanness and distinguishing our ancestors from other primate species.

BODY LANGUAGE

Although we humans are rather unique animals in so far as we have a large brain and we can speak to each other, as well as read and reason, it must be remembered that our ability to speak, read and reason is, in evolutionary terms, a recent development, and the majority of our communication with other members of the species is still the language of the body.

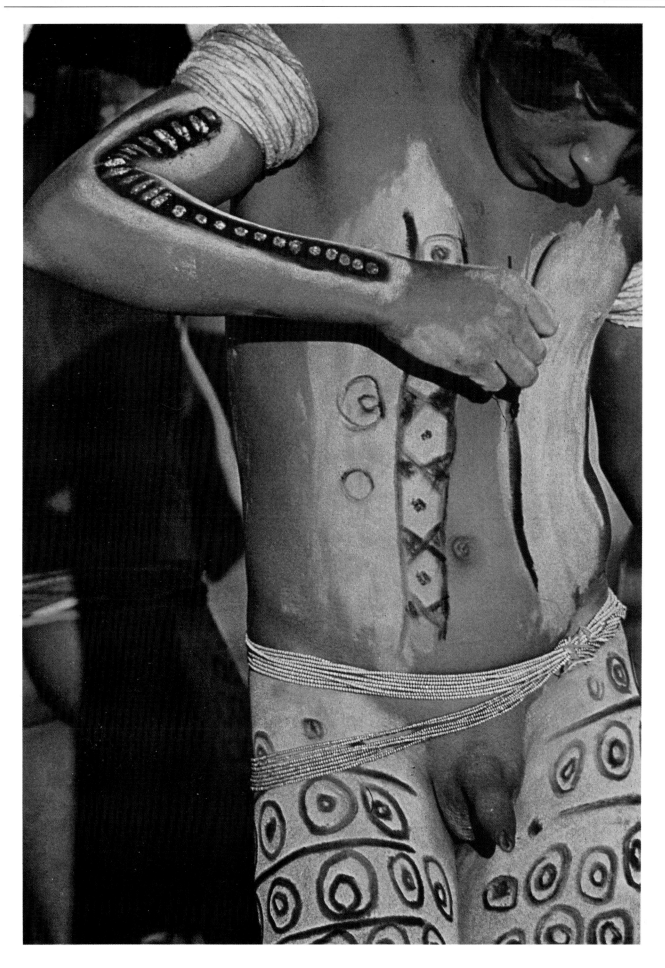

Research on this subject carried out by Professor Whistell and Albert Mehrabian shows that the total impact of a particular message is only about 7% verbal, whilst 93% is still communicated by predominately pre-human methods of expression. Of that primitive 93%, 38% is vocal — the tone, inflections and volume of the sounds but not the words themselves — and 55% is entirely non-verbal, which means that our primary means of communication is through facial expression, gesture and the way we present and package our bodies. Much of our body language is culturally taught rather than biologically inherited and in spite of belonging to a common primitive past it differs, like spoken language, from region to region, from society to society.

THE CULTURAL CONTEXT

We know from intensive research that members of a particular society share certain basic attitudes towards the human body, and that in any society there is a shared belief of how a beautiful, an erotic or a healthy body is defined. This means that the social body of a particular society has an influence on the way the sexual or the physical body is perceived. This is why we tend to perceive people of a different culture or race as looking alike. People of other races feel the same about us. And however hard people try to assert their individuality within that culture, the individual differences are lost on the outsider because they are only meaningful to those within.

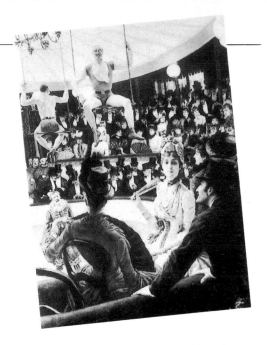

▲▶ *Differing cultural groups affirm their masculinity and femininity in different ways. The western woman may choose wigs, corsets, tight clothes and cosmetics and the African girl may choose mud and oil and scars and beads. Methods differ but the message is the same*

▼ *The symbolic garb of the High Court Judge speaks for itself, and whether the person wearing it is a crusty old man or an attractive woman, the air of authority surrounds them just as convincingly*

▼ *Looking alike, acting alike — Himmler and SS leaders in 1933*

▲ *A certain smile, an appealing gesture and a suggestive garment add up to an open invitation without a word being spoken*

MASCULINE OR FEMININE?

We all tend to cling to recognised symbols of maleness and femaleness, regarding them as specific attributes which express the masculine or feminine qualities of the individual, even if we disagree about what these attributes might be. For instance what we now regard as a symbol of femininity — such as wearing decorative dress, cosmetics, and jewellery — is seen in some cultures as a symbol of masculinity because in those cultures it is the accepted practice that only men wear such finery. However, not only do such symbols differ cross-culturally, but they also differ within a society from one period to another. Today the lace-trimmed garments of 17th and 18th century male aristocrats seem effeminate and foppish, whilst during these periods even the most masculine of men who could afford to do so, dressed in these styles.

▲ Male member of the Soma tribe, Western Province, New Guinea

▲▲ Symbols of belonging: extravagant facial hair and a wasp waist to exaggerate that manly chest

▲ Hip aprons worn by married women from Tugela Ferry, South Africa

▲▲ *Xinguano Indians from the Mato Grosso region of Brazil. The young girls [top], naked except for their body paint, have a strict code about who can touch who, and where. The young girls with hip bands are drawing attention to their newly-acquired sexual maturity*

◀ *Sikh men distinguish themselves from other Indian castes by their fine crop of perfectly groomed facial hair, and by their magnificent turbans. Sikhs never cut their head hair, they wear it knotted on the top of their heads which adds to their height and hence their personal esteem*

SYMBOLS OF BELONGING

As you can see, in trying to take stock of the human body in regard to its symbolic significance both socially and sexually, we are faced with a bewildering array of apparently contradictory evidence. This is because all such outward symbols are in fact symbols of our *humanness* and are not confined by nature to any one culture or sex. This is why humans all over the world spend so much time and energy adorning and decorating their bodies in such a large variety of ways. It is a human trait to wish to change our animal bodies into an acceptable *social body* and it is a human trait to so adorn that social body in a cultural style that clearly distinguishes it from those of its neighbours.

But despite all our frenzied attempts to make our bodies look different one from another, making use of various cultural badges, body customs, modes of behaviour and styles of sexual disparity, we are still the same basic human animals who inhabited the earth 25,000 years ago. Although we may have different-coloured skin, different facial features and varying sexual attributes, we still share a common heritage. And we have much more in common with one another than many people would like to admit.

ETHNIC BODY DECORATION

On my travels around the world, seeing at first hand the wide variety of body adornments and clothing styles worn by divergent ethnic groups, I found a surprising number of people in different parts of the world living perfectly normal lives whilst near naked; some wearing only plaited string thigh bands, beaded necklaces, feathered headdresses, or small fringed aprons that were worn at the back of the hips leaving their primary sexual areas completely exposed to view.

We are lucky that such cultures still exist. Eighteenth and 19th century missionaries and colonial administrators were blissfully blind to their own religious, cultural and sexual prejudices, and to the symbolism of their own tribal adornments — their tightly-laced corsets, powdered wigs, constricting shoes and styles of outer garments totally unsuited to colonial life. These missionaries and administrators nevertheless took it upon themselves to expunge all those "pagan, barbaric and savage forms of body packaging" which did not conform to their body covering standards. Because they believed that their own tribal customs had been ordained by God, the missionaries banned the tribal customs of others under threat of physical

punishment, and in some cases even death. Thus the social and symbolic significance of these traditional forms of body decoration which had evolved over countless generations, were, in many cases, destroyed forever. However, we can piece together a fascinating picture from areas of the world untouched by colonialism.

BODY PAINTING

The ancient art of body painting using natural materials such as coloured clays, pieces of ground-up rock, human saliva and the juice from berries is certainly among the oldest of human aesthetic activities, pre-dating cave painting, music, dance and religion by many thousands of years.

The 19th century colonials, of course, condemned native body painting as a pagan and barbaric custom, accentuating nakedness, lacking any sense of Christian modesty and encouraging sexual promiscuity. Fortunately in more recent times people have come to realize that body painting, like western-style clothing, was just another manifestation of the human desire to belong to a particular cultural group. And after much study, anthropologists like James Teit declared that body painting had great cultural, social, religious and sexual significance. Writing on the styles of body painting used by the native Indians of British Columbia he concluded that: "much of it was ornament, but much also had a strong connection with religion, dreams, guardian spirits, cure of disease, protection, prayers, speech, good luck, war and death." And he went on to say that when the young Indians painted themselves "it was usually to fascinate the opposite sex". Professor Favis supported this point of view about body painting in his book *Nuba Personal Art* (1972), in which he says that the decoration "is to accentuate the beauty of the body — they view their art only in relation to their bodies. The body is regarded by them as the consummation of Nuba art." And he too regarded sexual attraction as an essential ingredient in such an art form.

TATTOOING

Body paint washes off, tattooing on the other hand, being an indelible and permanent form of body decoration, cannot be removed without ugly scarring and is therefore used to denote an undeniably permanent change of status such as sexual maturity or marriage.

The art of tattooing was known to the Egyptians over 5000

▲▲▶ *A desire to attract the opposite sex: a young, wasp-waisted dandy from the Mekeo tribe of Melanesia, a group of Maasai warriors, grooming and decorating one another and [below opposite] a young 'flapper' painting her face*

years ago when dancers, singers and concubines were tattooed with the symbol of their divine protector *Bes*. Despite the passage of time, some forms of tattooing still retain the symbolic association of this early use.

From Egypt, the practice of tattooing appears to have spread along the trade routes to the South Pacific and Japan, and also into Europe and the British Isles. Julius Caesar commented on this practice after visiting parts of the British Isles. He described how part of that country was "occupied by barbarians who bear on their bodies coloured scars ingeniously formed in the likeness of various animals." In fact the word Briton is thought to relate to our ancestors' use of woad and tattooing — deriving as it does from the Breton term meaning "painted and patterned in colours."

With the arrival in Rome of many tattooed, fair-haired, and blue-eyed concubines from the new British colony, the art of tattooing became quite fashionable until it was suppressed by Emperor Constantine in AD325 on the request of the then immensely powerful Christian leaders, on the grounds that it was "a symbol of base sexuality". They also claimed that it disfigured that which was "fashioned in God's image". And as with many other forms of personal adornment and decoration, the art of tattooing was totally suppressed, and was rediscovered by the Renaissance traders in the 15th century along their trading routes in the South Pacific.

But it was the opening up of the Pacific Ocean in the late-18th century by Captain Cook, and of mainland Japan by Commodore Perry in the mid-19th century, which brought tattooing once again to the foreground of western fashion. George V was tattooed whilst still the Duke of York. His brother the Duke of Clarence was also tattooed as was Tsar Nicholas of Russia and many ladies of the various royal courts, including the famous American beauty Lady Randolph Churchill. Their tattoos (although quite pallid in comparison with those of the Maoris and the Japanese) were, nevertheless, a symbol of their daring and independence. Amongst the Polynesians and Maoris, tattooing was a symbol of sexual maturity and of individual rank. Young girls on reaching puberty and young boys after they had completed the arduous initiation ceremony, were tattooed in some specific way. The great chiefs had their faces and their bodies covered with designs of great intricacy and beauty and their facial tattoos became a kind of personal signature. In fact when the Maoris signed deeds of land sales to the early European settlers they frequently drew their face

▲▲ *A sense of belonging: a group of Japanese children, photographed in Kyoto in 1920 and members of the Gilles guild parading at the traditional Binche Carnival in Belgium, both are dressed in their unique medieval finery*

pattern instead of signing their name or making a cross. The faces of Maori women were also intricately tattooed, particularly on the lips and chin and they regarded a naked face as unattractive, old and ugly.

In Japan *irezumi* (their form of polychrome tattooing) reached its height of aesthetic expression during the *Edo* period (1615-1868). The wealthy merchants were not permitted to wear elaborately-decorated kimonos, fine silks, brocades, or gold jewellery as these were reserved by law for the ruling classes. They could, however, express their wealth and their independence by wearing an expensive secret tattoo under a plain kimono. This was displayed when bathing with friends — a national pastime — or when visiting the pleasure district. The prints and erotic drawings of this period rarely depict an unadorned naked body.

The Japanese have kept their love for *irezumi*. The coloured tattoos act as a form of decorative clothing, rendering the naked

▲▲ *The illustration [left] is from Ivan Krunsenstern's book* Voyage Round the World *(1813) and shows the intricate tatoos of a Nakahira chief from the Pacific Islands. The photograph [above] depicts not tattooing, but the ancient art of hennaing, much practised in India and the Middle East, where very intricate patterns are applied on the hands and the feet during times of celebration*

To be tattooed is a sign of nobility; not to be a sign to the contrary.
Herodotus

skin aesthetically appealing and sexually desirable. An un-tattooed, or unadorned body is still considered *naked*, and is therefore an unfit object for human passion.

MUTILATION

The choice of which part of the body a particular cultural group, traditionally decorates, exaggerates, or even mutilates is never random. Nor is the method used — based as it is upon the symbolic belief in the body as an essential and integral part of a culture. In all societies and cultural groups, particular areas of the human body will be stressed or altered in some way. Thus each group will mark their members as different from their neighbours, with a consistent trend throughout the world towards emphasising those particular physical attributes which are already noticeably different. This emphasis tends to make an individual more attractive to their own group, and less attractive to the neighbours.

The tradition in the western world for instance has been to admire a woman for her facial beauty, her neck and shoulders, the shape of her breasts and the narrowness of her waist, which for hundreds of years have been the focal point of our ideas of beauty. Other societies and cultural groups have developed other notions of beauty, placing the emphasis on the feminine foot, the shape of the buttocks, or the scar formations which have been applied to the body.

Some anthropologists believe that the Chinese *lotus* foot originated in those areas of China which bordered on to its warlike neighbours, the Tartars. The feet of females in these areas were naturally smaller than those of the Tartar women and, in order to make the young females less attractive to the Tartar hordes who were continually plundering that part of China, a system of foot binding to accentuate this natural characteristic was gradually introduced over the centuries by the wealthier members of Chinese society. M Bertin noted in *China, Its Costume, Arts and Manufactures* (1813) that the Tartars had the greatest contempt for the Chinese women, "particularly those who had small feet. They preferred women who gave their foot its natural length". To emphasise this feature the Tartar women "added to its length by wearing long curved shoes which the Chinese, in derision, called *Tartar Junks* from the resemblance they bear to these vessels".

Once the practice of foot-binding had started it became more elaborate and gradually spread throughout China, even though it had long outlived its original purpose. Gradually, the *lotus*

▲▲▲ *Various forms of mutilation — foot binding, circumcision and head-shaping — designed to pass on to infant members of the tribe the characteristics that will mark them as different from their neighbours*

foot became a symbol of prestige, wealth, and natural beauty, in much the same way as the tightly-bound whalebone corset had become a similar symbol in mid-19th century Europe. In both cases, the woman is obviously unfit for work and this greatly increases her value as a showcase for wealth. It also allowed her to devote her time to looking attractive and to learning the arts of pleasure.

Interestingly enough, in both cases the parents of the girls who were to have their waists or their feet bound were themselves reasonably wealthy, otherwise they would have been unable to afford the expense involved, not to mention losing the asset of an extra pair of employable hands. In fact, in China, the expense of foot binding was considerably more than that involved in western waist binding, as a specialist had to be employed each day to attend to the girl's feet to prevent sores or even gangrene from setting in and the feet had to be re-bound each day for up to eight years to achieve the *lotus* shape desired.

This process of binding and lacing greatly increased the risk of death and disease of the young female population during this period. Some experts, Alison Lurie included, believe that this risk heightens the erotic appeal of such fashions: "One of the most persistent specialised forms of erotic appeal" she wrote in 1982, "is that which connects love and death, sometimes so closely that only what is damaged or dangerous can arouse the passions." She noted that in 19th century Europe, "the sexual instinct and the death-wish were often intertwined." Not only were frailty and delicacy admired but

▲ Sufferers of pulmonary tuberculosis, or consumption, as it was commonly known in the 19th century, could find themselves the object of much erotic interest. The disease was believed to arouse a 'feverish sensuality' and bring a sexual glow to the face of the patient

▲ Body hair has distinct sexual significance, some groups are quite happy with it, and it makes others feel distinctly uncomfortable. The removal of body hair is a social practice, it is done so that the individual will fit in to the required pattern. One such casualty was Johnny Weissmuller's chest, which was shaved and oiled daily

◀ The removal of head hair is seen as a form of punishment, or as a demeaning act. Army recruits have their hair shorn to indicate their subservience to authority, monks have the crowns of their heads shaved for much the same reason. After World War II many collaborators had their hair shaved off before being escorted out of town, as shown in Robert Capa's poignant 1944 photograph

she thought that for many the actual illness itself "was sexually exciting". And she continued: "the favoured disease was pulmonary tuberculosis, the high fever of which brought a hectic flush to the cheeks and brightness to the eyes, mimicking sexual arousal; it was also believed to produce an unearthly and feverish sensuality in both sexes."

Today, of course, we tend to think of such forms of perversity and mutilation as uncivilized and even barbaric, yet we condone circumcision and plastic surgery, both of which are used simply to make individuals into acceptable social beings.

Some anthropologists believe that like the origins of foot binding, the wearing of lip plugs by various cultural groups in Africa, and parts of the Amazon region of South America also originally came about as a visual safety device to ward off evil spirits and the possibility of local kidnappers or slave-traders. It is believed that the cultural groups who originally wore these lip plugs had slightly more protuberant lips than their neighbours, which they made more protuberant as a form of protection from evil spirits. With the growth of the slave trade however, those who wore lip plugs were virtually unsaleable and therefore not worth kidnapping — a good enough reason to increase the size of the lip plugs and for more communities to adopt their use. And the tradition has continued until the present day.

The lip plugs are therefore an essential symbol of tribal salvation and are as important to the communities who still wear them as skullcaps are to the Orthodox Jews and rosary beads to the Catholics.

Head shapes have also been in and out of fashion. In ancient Egypt a long narrow head was much admired, as it was in France in the 18th century when it was commonly thought that a long narrow head was a sign of great intelligence and there was much head binding of infants. Again in Germany in the 1930s infant head binding and skull manipulation was much practiced, not so much to get a long narrow head but to avoid having a child with a round head which was racially frowned upon as a sign of Jewishness.

Other groups of people in other parts of the world flatten their already flat noses because it makes them look more attractive to their peers. Others enlarge their already large earlobes so that they can drape them enticingly for others to admire. Others stretch and distort the neck with wide neckbands of heavy metal, or tightly bind their upper arms or their thighs.

▲▲ *Mutilation courtesy of the plastic surgeon's knife. Michael Jackson has undergone extensive surgery to alter the shape of his nose, lips, jaw and cheekbones in order to become, as it says in the press handouts, "more aesthetic and more attractive to his fans"*

▲ *Intricate bas-relief scarification typical of the Nuba of the Sudan*

SCARIFICATION

At one time there was a fashion for duelling scars, and even today sporting scars are still much admired in some circles. The broken nose of a rugby player, for instance, gives him social status within the rugby fraternity and it has been known for some players to refuse medical assistance in having their nose re-set, or a scar surgically repaired, as this would lead to loss of status.

Elsewhere various forms of scarification are inflicted upon an individual as a clear and visible symbol of their allegiance to a particular cultural group, and their social standing within that group. In many tribal communities in Africa, a particular form of scar patterning is used to denote a rite of passage such as when a girl reaches puberty, or when a boy becomes a warrior — in much the same indelible way as a tattoo. In

▲▲ *Decorative scaring and sharpened teeth adorn these natives of the Northern Congo [top]. In the west, scars are a badge of courage or a testament to a racy past, rather than a mark of beauty. The gentleman photographed here bears his duelling scars with considerable pride*

▶ *Light-skinned races, like the Berbers, rarely use scaring as a tribal decoration, preferring to adorn themselves with tattoos and with paint*

Clothes resemble a perpetual blush upon the surface of humanity.
Prof. J C Flugel *1930*

fact it has been noted that tribal scarification is only used on the dark pigmented skins which do not show tattoos to advantage. Where the racial pigmentation is naturally lighter, such as amongst the Berber tribe of the northern areas of the Sahara, tattooing takes the place of tribal scars, clearly distinguishing the Berbers from their darker-skinned neighbours.

Many tribal scars are in fact a sort of bas-relief tattoo, in which the skin is pierced with a sharp hooked thorn to lift the skin and pull it up so that it can be cut with a small blade on the top edge of the raised section. The resulting cut is then rubbed with a mixture of fruit juices and ground ash so that the cut becomes inflamed and later heals as a hard scar in relief.

Another form of traditional tribal scarification is that known as *cicatrization* — a scar formed by carefully cutting the surface of the skin into the traditional design required, easing the wound apart slightly, and then inflaming it with ground ash, so that a flat shiny scar forms.

The large raised *keloids*, used to outline the facial features of some tribal members, are a particularly dramatic form of scar caused by aggravating the wounds in a special way during the healing process with a mixture of acidic fruit juices and ash so that they become much more pronounced than the *cicatrization* scars.

In addition to the symbolic meaning of scars, they also have the added bonus of being a form of preventive medicine which in fact probably accounts for the survival of this practice. The body gradually builds up anti-bodies during the scaring process so that the mature adult is able to survive in the harsh conditions of bush life. On maturity, many adults add to their traditional patterning of scars for purely decorative reasons and to mark them out as attractive individuals worthy of the attention of members of the opposite sex. When the American anthropologist Paul Bohannan asked a particular member of the *Tiv* tribe of Nigeria in the mid-1970s if such additional scaring was painful, he replied, "Of course it is painful. What girl would look at a man if his scars had not cost him pain?" The women also suffer pain during this final decorative scarring process. Leni Riefenstahl in *People of Kau* (1976) explains that, despite the pain, the woman being decorated rarely cries out: "the extent of her self control can only be gauged from an occasional tremor on her face." And she goes on to say that although many women lose a great deal of blood during the scarring process, and some even lose consciousness, the rewards are high. "The new patterns that adorn her body render a female Nuba highly attractive to the opposite sex and enrol her among the most desirable women in her village."

IT'S MAGIC!

Our ancestors wore animal skins while out hunting in order to get near to the animals without being noticed, and as time passed the skins themselves gained a symbolic and mystical significance quite separate from their origins. Body painting, carved masks, and an assortment of adornments gradually replaced the original animal skins and eventually the stylized artifacts took on an almost sacred meaning. This is still true today. Clothes and ornaments can be magical, they can mark out the holy, the successful warrior, the social lion and the social pariah.

TROPHIES

Anthropologists refer to the wearing of an animal skin by a successful hunter as an ancient form of trophism that serves to testify to that individual's skill and courage. Successful hunters festooned their bodies with claws, tusks, teeth and tails of the more notable animals they had killed, and some warriors did likewise with various parts taken from the bodies of slain warriors they had killed in battle. Some forms of symbolic trophism were used during Greek and Roman times when military heroes would be adorned with leopard or cheetah skins as a less gruesome substitute for human scalps or a dead warrior's once virile member.

Even today, the wearing of a distinct mark associated with the killing of enemy warriors still lingers on in the custom for wearing medals to commemorate famous battles or as an award for valour in the face of the enemy. In fact the gold braided epaulets, swags, sashes, tassels and other adornments which festoon the ceremonial dress of military leaders are the symbolic remnants of some long forgotten kill.

EMBLEMS

All styles of dress which symbolise a recognizable occupation, activity or belief are emblematic. Hence a policeman's uniform is emblematic, as are official school uniforms, the livery worn by athletic teams, the uniforms worn by boy scouts and girl guides, the style of dress traditionally worn by wine waiters or chefs and those worn by air hostesses.

▲▲▲ *The emblematic uniform: from the top, Eric von Stroheim in a Hollywood version of a military uniform, the ubiquitous French maid and the updated nun's habit, an effort to move with the times that backfired*

The forbidden modes of attire worn by the members of the Ku Klux Klan are emblematic, as are those worn by other secret societies such as the Freemasons, and the religious vestments worn by the Pope, a Bishop or other ecclesiastics. The formal robes of the judiciary are designed as emblems of office and even the traditional business suit is considered emblematic by many contemporary writers.

The purpose of these forms of dress is to identify the wearer as a member of specific group, and often to locate that wearer within the hierarchy of that group. Sometimes we are being given information about the wearer's individual achievements such as with the merit badges of a scout or guide, the crossed rifles of the marksmen on a military uniform or the wings worn by an airline pilot. When we think of a nurse, or a nun or a judge for example, we usually conjure up a specific image. We don't usually see a person in our imaginations, we see their clothes, and by their clothes we know them.

Generally most emblematic styles, when first introduced, are of their time and so are easy to read in the sartorial language of that time. But like all official styles they tend to become frozen in time and dated unless they are upgraded. However it is in this area of upgrading that most problems befall emblematic styles. Over time these styles become associated with a mixture of ideas, incorporating the wearers' and the observers' expectations of the visual message they transmit. In the early 1970s many uniforms — police, military, fire brigade etc. — were completely re-designed in a drive for efficiency. Yet efficiency had a very low priority in the minds of the wearers, who were prepared to undergo a great deal of discomfort in order to project the visual image they had of themselves in the uniform. What was wanted was not comfort but a visual statement which would declare the wearer an adult and create an *esprit de corps*. Wherever the new, ergonomic uniforms were introduced, there was a marked drop in recruitment and in morale.

Another example of a different kind which will illustrate the complexity of such modes of dress was the introduction of an updated version of a nun's habit, a mode of dress which although basically emblematic in concept had become, in the eyes of the public, one involving a great deal of status (even though the nun's habit had evolved from a very lowly mode of dress). Over time the habit had taken on a very specific meaning in the eyes of the public, and to change its style risked losing the message it transmitted. Nevertheless the decision

▲▼ *Warding off the evil eye [above] with cowrie shells, long associated with the female vulva and therefore fertility, and [below] Tiwa Indians of New Mexico, to whom mere splendour is not enough; their adornment becomes ritual heraldry and a form of visual language in itself*

▲ *The Spanish lace mantilla was traditionally worn as a form of protection from the tempting glances of a potential seducer, and the ravages of the hot sun. Eventually the mantilla itself became a symbol of protection from evil*

▼ *An emblematic mode of attire designed to strike fear into the heart of the outsider and deny the individuality of the wearer — the hooded robes of the Ku Klux Klan*

▲▼ *Facial decoration to ward off evil spirits and frighten the enemy*

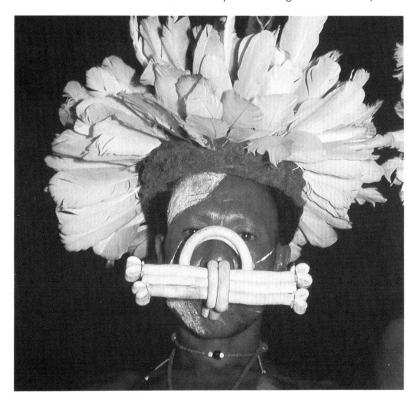

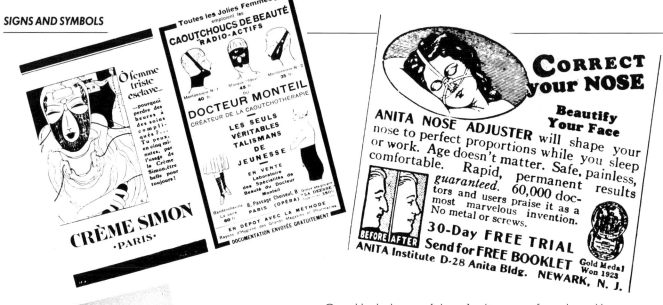

▼▼▲▲ Good luck charms: [above] talismans of youth and beauty, [left] a 'skeleton' pattern of braid [bottom] magic lip plug

was taken to upgrade and bring the habit into line with modern concepts of dress, in the hope that it would bring nuns and the people closer together.

The new style habit, which looked like a black version of a nurse's uniform, totally de-frocked them in the religious sense. Without their flowing robes the faithful did not feel the same way about them, they had lost their status and their recruitment levels fell dramatically.

WARDING OFF THE EVIL EYE

Professor Flugel raises the question of the influence of magic and of the evil eye on our ancestors' styles of dress and decoration, and he suggests that amulets and some forms of clothing and decoration were used "to ward off the evil influences of unwelcome spirits," namely accidents, disease, death and infertility which were thought to have been the work of the evil eye.

One of the reasons why so many ancient amulets appear to be symbols of the male and female reproductive organs was because one of the chief ways in which the evil eye was supposed to harm its victims was by rendering them infertile. This close magical association between the shape of the human sexual organs and the protective powers of early amulets is also related to the use of phallic symbolism in dress. On this point Professor Flugel suggests: "It would appear that the general sexual symbolism of clothes, in virtue of which clothes seem to form an unconscious substitute for crude sexual display, is reinforced by the magical exhibition of sexual symbols as a defence against the fear of infertility." And this association between magical symbolism and sexual display is generally acknowledged by most other sartorial experts and by many designers of contemporary fashion.

Certain forms of decoration were used to increase an individual's fertility by "pleasing the Gods". Cowrie shells have been widely used for tens of thousands of years in many forms of decoration as symbols of fertility because of their close visual association with the female genitals. Certain forms of ethnic scarring seem to have evolved because of the belief in their magical quality for increasing an individual's fertility. This is why scarification is often linked to the onset of puberty.

If we look at the current array of western cosmetics and modes of body decoration through the eyes of an anthropologist we can see that the way in which they are used is also closely related to magical fertility rituals. Today, many people regard loosing their youthful looks as the greatest evil they have to face, and to them cosmetics and hair colourants hold the key to overcoming this evil. For others the magic may be a new hat, a new pair of shoes or a new outfit.

Many sociologists are now realizing that this form of magic is a liberating force, and instead of attacking new fashions and the use of cosmetics as being frivolous and elitist as they did in the past, they now realize that they have as deep a symbolic meaning for people from the industrialised world as they do for other tribal groups.

INVOKING SUPERNATURAL POWERS

Certain forms of facial decoration, necklaces of shark's teeth, girdles made with animal claws, and bracelets, anklets and other adornments are supposed to have magical qualities. Polynesian islanders perforate the septum of the nose and insert a decorative bone as a magic ritual to secure eternal happiness. Others tattoo their skins with certain patterns to "please their god *Dengei*". In parts of New Guinea, in order to invoke magical forces to help overcome an adversary, boar's tusks and cassowary quills are worn through holes in the nostrils and cheeks. Some societies use particular symbols in their mode of body painting to bring good luck and to protect the wearer whilst partaking in a lion hunt. Others use special modes of adornment at seasonal feasts to ensure a good harvest. And still others decorate and adorn themselves in special ways when going into battle to be sure of success by invoking the help of their warrior ancestors.

Particular forms of clothing may be reserved for use only in a religious ceremony, to put the wearers in direct contact

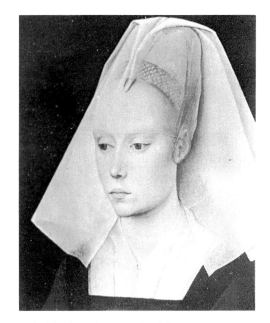

▲ *In Medieval times a high brow was considered a fortunate feature and was emphasised by plucking out the eyebrows*

▲ *It is possible that the idea of the corset developed somewhere in the Middle East about 10,000 years ago among the poor, who bound their waists and stomachs to stop them feeling the pain of hunger, and that once introduced it became a symbol of survival for these people, and in time it was seen as an attractive adornment*

Nations attach the idea of beauty to everything which particularly characterizes their own physical conformation, their natural physiognomy.
Alexander von Humboldt *1814*

A brief fashion statement in a shape, a size, a color for everybody.

Both cotton rib and jungle prints available in low rise and string bikini styles.

PLAYBOY BRIEFS

Dressing for success: Young men preparing for a night on the town. Businessmen preparing to do their best often cleanse and clothe themselves to a ritual pattern in order to psych themselves up. The man near-left gains confidence knowing that, concealed beneath his business suit, is an impressive lucky tattoo

Rites of passage Nuba style: in the southern Sudanese province of Kordofan, the young unmarried males of the South East Nuba tribe partake in a knife-fighting display in order to attract a wife or a lover. After the fight, the men sit in a circle and the young women dance around them. Each girl will then choose a mate by marking him with the scent of her vulva

Rites of passage western style: Until recently, progress through life was marked by various events: baptism, confirmation, marriage and so on, each of which required a special outfit. Baptism and confirmation dresses [far left] have always been white, signifying purity, but wedding dresses in some western cultures — the one on the left was photographed in Hungary in the 1920s — were bright and colourful

with the magical powers of their god. And in some religions these special garments also act as a magical protection against moral danger. The power of magical protection against the lures and temptations of the world inherent in religious raiments are used by many Christian priests to avoid the distracting influences that might lead them away from the straight and narrow path of virtue. Their example may also be followed by some pious members of the congregation who will tend to wear all-enveloping garments. The wearing of the cross also originated as a means of protecting the wearers from evils associated with the Devil and his minions. Witch doctors wear a whole array of magical adornments, some of which actually seem to work, a powerful example of mind over matter.

In many places of the world people pick out the lines of their ribs with white clay or paint as a form of magical symbol. This practice of converting the living body into a *skeleton spectre* is fired by the belief that in this way they can call on the power of their dead ancestors and the spirits of the underworld. In fact, it is believed that the rib-like chest-braiding on military uniforms, including those worn by the cadets at West Point and the British Hussars, originated in this way, being originally a visual device to give the wearer great courage and at the same time to frighten the enemy.

GOOD LUCK CHARMS

Soldiers have traditionally worn items of clothing borrowed from their loved ones as a form of lucky charm when going into battle. Howell wrote in his *Familiar Letters* (1627) concerning one of the many battles between the French and the English fought at that time: "A captain told me that when they were rifling the dead bodies of the French gentlemen after the first invasion they found that many of them had their mistress's favours tied about their genitories."

The male members of the Mambas tribe who live in the New Hebrides often wrap their penises in many yards of calico, winding and folding this until it is a neat bundle some 18 inches/45 cm long by about 3 inches/7 cm wide — not out of modesty, but to protect their virile member from the effects of *Narak*. And the *Peguans* of South Burma used to wear bells tied to the penis so that the sound would protect them from any evil spirits. This is also said to be the reason why many warriors of New Guinea and Borneo wear colourful gourd penis sheaths which protect the penis but leave the testicles exposed as they do not believe these are in danger.

The practice of wrapping the genitals in an item of clothing borrowed from a loved one had, by the 17th century, become one of the most powerful of all protective symbols, and is still practised today, not only to ward off the evil eye, or the effects of death and disease, but also as a good luck charm.

Sportsmen on the other hand may put their faith in a pair of 'lucky' shoes, a 'lucky' sweater or a 'lucky' cap. Many footballers have a special ritual for preparing their boots before a big match: Tottenham Hotspur's miracle goal scorer Jimmy Greaves is said to have used a secret formula in the preparation of his boots, to have worn special socks and to have tied his boot laces in a particular way. Many actresses believe ardently in the magical power of a 'lucky' piece of clothing which they wear when auditioning or performing, and when this particular item is beyond repair they still insist on taking it with them to each performance. The orchestral conductor Leonard Bernstein, until very recently always wore a pair of "lucky" cufflinks when conducting.

Many gamblers believe certain items of apparel bring them good luck. And some fashion designers refuse to use certain colour combinations in their shows, not because they are aesthetically displeasing or do not sell, but because they are considered 'unlucky'.

At weddings it is traditional for the bride to wear a veil which shields her from the harmful effects of evil spirits on the way to the church. The white wedding dress itself is also regarded as having magical qualities: cancelling out the bride's previous sexual experiences so that she may enter marriage as a symbolic virgin, if not a physical one.

A RITUAL OF SELF CONFIDENCE

South Pacific traders wear special styles of clothing and use a range of specially-prepared natural oils, herbs and paints, which they refer to as magical aids, to make themselves and their merchandise irresistible to the inhabitants of the island they are visiting.

The South Pacific islander is, in essence, no different from his western counterpart who prepares himself for an important sales meeting by carrying out his own preparatory ritual of cleaning his teeth, shaving, applying a fragrant aftershave and deodorant, putting on a business suit, clean shirt, tie and polished shoes. This ritual gives the businessman a feeling of self confidence which will favourably influence his behaviour at the scheduled sales meeting.

▲▲ The white wedding dress became fashionable only about 100 years ago when brides felt the need to publicly reinforce their virgin status. The coronation of a monarch is again a rite of passage. Queen Elizabeth II asked her dressmaker, Norman Hartnell, to incorporate into the dress all the emblems of her realm as a symbol of regal power

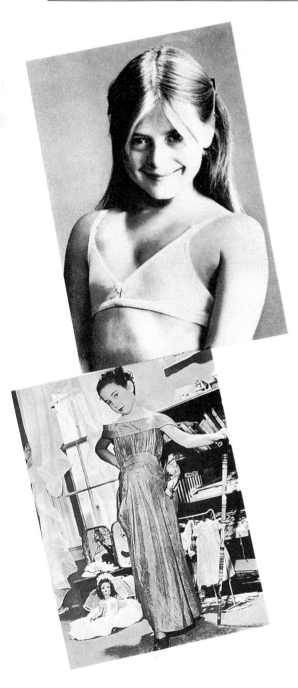

▲▲ *Children all over the world love to dress up and emulate the grown-ups. Little girls look forward to wearing bras and high-heeled shoes and so manufacturers came up with the 'pre-teen bra' and 'junior miss heels', leaving precious little in the way of symbolic clothing to mark the age of puberty*

A MARK OF PROGRESS

All societies mark the progress of the individual through the milestones of life by visual coded messages. In the western world the church and the education system have been given the specific responsibility of marking most of these rites of passage by various ceremonial occasions such as baptism, confirmation and marriage on the one hand; and the graduation of classes through infants, junior, high school, college and university on the other. Each stage is traditionally marked by the wearing of specific types of garment: the christening dress of the baby, the confirmation outfit, the once-in-a-lifetime clothes worn by bride and groom. At school clothing regulations change as one progresses from infant to school leaver. At university, the conferring of a degree is marked by a cap and gown. Coronation robes display for all the world to see the full weight of regal power.

The purpose of these special clothes is to help us come to terms with each new situation and to fit into our new role in life. However, sometimes the need for the symbolism is even greater than the desire for the new status. Lee Comer suggests for instance in *Wedlocked Women* (1974), that for many young women their decision to get married revolves not so much around marrying the man of their dreams, but around "the dress, the flowers, the hymns, the guests and present list, the bridesmaids and the speeches and the whole display that attends the ritual."

SIGNS OF THE TIMES

Whether we realize it or not we have sensitively attuned notions of how we think people should look, and the boundaries are sufficiently well defined to alert us to the warning signs when the boundaries are breached. Some people however, the dropouts of our times according to Victoria Ebin in her book *The Body Decorated* (1979), "demonstrate their rejection of conventional values by their physical appearance — an act sometimes perceived by others as aggressive and therefore likely to elicit hostility." These individuals are in fact using the emotive power of symbolism to inform all others in their social group of two important facts: 1) They have reached the age of sexual maturity and 2) They are not prepared to accept the confines of the currently established mode.

It is well understood that it isn't the appearance of the actual clothes themselves which is of importance, but the coded language of defiance against those in authority which is at

▲ *The older generation often find it difficult to come to terms with new forms of dress, because they do not realise that all forms of dress are transitory, and just a sign of changing times*

▼ *During this century, many traditional modes of male dress have lost their inherent sexual symbolism as women have adopted them for their own wardrobes*

the root of such rebellious style. These styles are alive with signs, portents and an intriguing array of mixed metaphors, and they have sufficient troubling effect to make the law-makers leaf nervously through the statute books in an attempt find a legitimate reason to put a stop to it all.

A SHOW OF MATURITY

Sociobiologists tell us that there comes a time in every young girl's life when she has the inner desire to display her hidden physical charms in order to seek a mate and earn the admiration of her peers. Young males also reach a stage in their physical development when they wish to show their independence, and to visibly state that they are sexually mature and ready to seek a mate.

In the naked state, of course, all this would be obvious, but in clothed societies young girls have been persuaded to make displays of dress rather than of their natural physical charms and young men were offered the chance of wearing styles, previously denied to them, like long trousers, which denoted their new status as a man. This system of course broke down when prepubescent individuals were allowed to wear those styles of dress previously reserved for the sexually mature adult population.

Society, which was unable to offer its young people an alternative symbol of maturity, therefore prompted the newly-nubile into varying degrees of nudity, which clearly showed their newly acquired development, and into a variety of rebellious styles. How else could these new adults inform the rest of society that they were no longer children?

▲ *In the west, the law frowns upon open displays of nubile charms*

Similarly, as long trousers and neckties gradually became absorbed into women's wardrobes, they began to loose their phallic symbolism and many men became faced with the difficult problem of how to display their masculinity. This of course is an additional reason why an increasing number of young males wear the more outlandish styles of dress which have evolved in recent years.

What is not generally understood is that the same messages are also being transmitted by the various forms of body decoration used by young people who live in non-industrialized societies. The feather headdresses of the tribal warriors of the Highlands of New Guinea, the facial displays of bones, shells and quills by the warriors of Borneo, the hairstyles and beading of the Maasai youths, the neckbands of the *Chin* women from Padaung, the tattoos of the Polynesians, the cicatrization of the peoples of the Cameroons, the body painting patterns of the Australian aboriginals are all directly linked to displays of sexual maturity in exactly the same way as the use of cosmetics, the wearing of high-heeled shoes, being given one's first pair of long trousers, being shown how to shave, or any one of a dozen other things which occur between the ages of 12 and 16.

CODED SEXUAL MESSAGES

In different eras people have found different styles of body presentation, as well as different physical characteristics and body types sexually attractive. Although it is probably true to say that few key types ever go completely out of erotic fashion, many people are nevertheless embarked on a never-

▲ Fashionable proportions for bottoms change rapidly

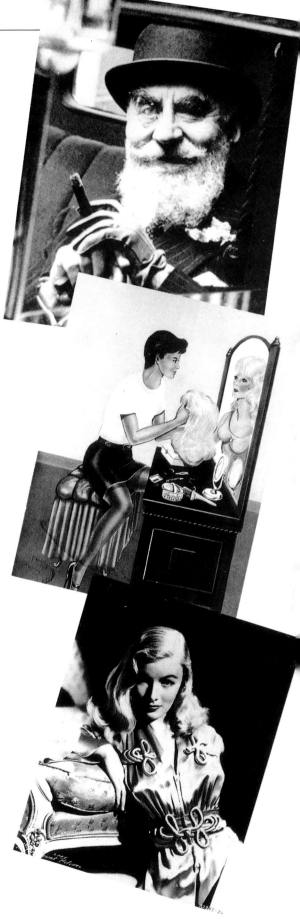

▲▲▲ Hair and gender: Facial hair has always been an undeniable male characteristic, whereas long, well-groomed head hair is now seen as distinctly feminine

ending search for the ideal form of physical attractiveness and the ideal package to show it off. As a result of the close association with certain parts of the body, various items of clothing and methods of body decoration have become imbued with erotic messages.

THE SHOE

Many writers and theoreticians have explored the apparent psychological connection between a small foot and a small vagina. Professor G Stanley Hall writing in *The American Journal of Psychology* at the turn of the century suggested that the shoe itself was a symbol of the female genitals, and that of all the forms of erotic symbolism, "the most frequent is that which idealizes the foot and the shoe." Havelock Ellis also discussed the erotic symbolism of both the male and female shoes in the first volume of his *Studies*, referring to the male shoe as a phallic symbol and the female shoe as a symbol of the female genitalia.

Bernard Rudofsky in the introduction to *The Unfashionable Human Body* (1972) showed how deeply ingrained this particular fetish is in our culture. "The tale of Cinderella," wrote Rudofsky, "is a veritable case history for the psychopathology of dress." He pointed out that the original story by the brothers Grimm had been greatly modified in most 20th century editions, omitting the details of the toe and heel amputations undertaken on the ugly sisters by their doting mother, so that one of them might become the bride of the prince. But the all-important point was that the gullible prince was willing to marry either of these ugly sisters until he spotted the blood. Only then did he meet Cinderella and love — equated by shoe size — eventually triumphed with the finding of the foot of his dreams. At the other end of the scale, of course, there's the old lady who had a shoe big enough to live in, probably because she had so many children she didn't know what to do.

Fine-spun ankles, small, pretty feet, flattered by her sheerest stockings and her high-heeled satin slippers, and the lacy hem of a ballet-length skirt

◀▲▼ *"Women who love shoes," it has been said, "know that life without the right shoes is a dull, lack-lustre expanse of grey days and sleepless nights."*

Give a girl the correct footwear and she can conquer the world.
Bette Midler *1983*

Many writers have suggested the reason for this erotic connection was that women's shoes show off to great advantage the foot, ankle and leg which are undoubtedly very important secondary sexual characteristics. This was particularly true during the 16th to 19th centuries when a glimpse of an ankle or a delicate shoe beneath the hem of a skirt reportedly "drove men to distraction" as it was "a symbol of the delights which were above". In her book *Shoes Never Lie* (1985) Mimi Pond suggests that shoes are "totems of disembodied lust. They are candy for the eyes, poetry for the feet, icing on your soul. They stand for everything you've ever wanted: glamour, success, a rapier-like wit, a date with the sex-god of your choice — they have the magic power to make you into someone else."

JEWELLERY

Taken in broad view, the absence of jewellery on the modern man of power and high status is strange as in the past men always marked their position in society with an ostentatious display of gold and precious stones. In the non-industrialized world it is the headman or successful hunters who wear most of the jewellery, while for us in the west, jewellery is almost entirely the prerogative of women.

Ethnic jewellery may be worn as a symbol of power to seek protection, luck, fertility or sexual allure. In western Europe too, in the Middle Ages, jewellery was worn for both magical and religious reasons, as well as for status and as a sexual lure. Many men used to wear earrings in the hope of improving their sight, to improve their virility or to prevent disease. In the church a bishop wore a sapphire ring as an emblem of chastity — a practice which survives to this day. Early Egyptian jewellery was almost entirely devoted to magic, religion and symbols of state. Much Minoan and Mycenaean jewellery had magical, sexual and religious significance, whilst the jewellery of classical Greece seems to have been more related to social position and wealth which, as I have pointed out earlier, is a powerful aphrodisiac. And what is the message from today's jewel-laden? More of the same: I belong; I am lucky; I am beautiful; I am loved and admired; I have wealth and power.

Earrings and necklaces also have the added allure of making the wearer more body conscious. When sexually aroused, the human face undergoes certain changes, one of these changes is to the earlobes which become engorged with blood. This physiological state is enhanced, or mimicked, by the use of

▲▲▲ *What lies behind shoe fetishism is the symbolic link between small female feet and the size of the vagina*

▲ *Jewellery of an explicitly sexual nature from Africa*

▲ *A glimpse of stocking and petticoat from 18thC France*

▲ *Taken in the broad view, jewellery is undoubtedly very sexual and very elitist in intent, its main aim being to display wealth and social position whilst at the same time drawing the observer's eye to the erogenous zones and to heighten the body-awareness of the wearer*

earrings which tend to make the ears slightly red due to the pressure of the clip and movement of the earring — or just by the wearer being physically conscious of the ears often induces a localized blush. Long drop earrings which gently stroke the neck, and the wearing of a necklace is also sexually stimulating, as the neck is an important erogenous zone and the sexual stimulation is often reflected in the face or eyes of the wearer.

LINGERIE AND LACE

"In future we will avoid all references to ladies' under-linen because the treatment of this subject calls for minutiae of detail which is extremely offensive to refined and sensitive women."
The Ladies Home Journal (Philadelphia 1898)

The 'unmentionable' open-legged drawers which originated in Venice during the 17th century were originally worn only by courtesans, but their use quickly spread throughout Europe where they were worn by both courtesans and prostitutes until the early 19th century when the more adventurous 'actresses' and 'dancers' adopted them as an essential part of their sexual armoury. By the mid-19th century these garments had been transformed by the use of frills and lace edging which also decorated the multitudinous layers of petticoats. The merest glimpse of these frilly edgings of lace became synonymous with sexual excitement. By the early 1920s the sale of modified and streamlined versions of lace-edged undergarments — now known as lingerie — had spread throughout the western world replacing the plain linen and flannel petticoats and untrimmed open-legged 'unmentionables' which had gradually become popular towards the end of the 19th century. And it seems that these new garments had been imbued with the power to evoke a narcissistic pleasure in the wearer and erotic feelings in the observer. Many lovers have confessed that the mere glimpse of a forbidden section of lace edging or lingerie frill "is often more sexually exciting than the sight of the genital region itself".

In fact lace edging possess such a high biological and psychological significance for some that the merest glimpse has been shown to give many young men an instantaneous erection. And writers like Prudence Glynn acknowledge that frills have become a sexual tease "signifying the pubic hair and the labia in the minds of many people".

If recent revelations made by several bespoke tailors from London's West End are to be believed, a surprising number of men also wear lace-trimmed silk undergarments as a foil to their rather military-style hand-tailored suits. We are told they wear these garments to excite the women in their lives. And in America research undertaken by several mail order companies specialising in women's lingerie showed that a noticeable proportion of sales were special orders in men's sizes. In response to demand they now carry silk, lace and frilled lingerie in men's fittings, together with a range of men's laced-up corsets, stockings and suspender belts not, as one would imagine, for the gay market but for sale to normal married businessmen who need an erotic release from the pressures of their work, or who have grown tired of clinical sex.

COSMETICS

Five thousand years ago, the ancient Egyptians were blackening their eyelashes with kohl, painting their faces with galena, dying their greying hair and wearing wigs imported from India. Cleopatra is reputed to have used rare perfumes in greater quantity than any other woman before or since.

The Sumerians are known to have painted round their eyes with powdered malachite and tinted their cheeks with red dyes. The Minoans used facial make-up, perfumes and a delightful mixture of opium, gall of a black ox, rat's urine, a scorpion

▲▲▲ Promises, promises: lace underclothing had sinful connections with the demi-mondaines and the can-can dancers. Madame de Pompadour's extravagant bows were there for the undoing. Cosmetics promised to transform the plainest Jane into a Goddess of Love

▲ The excitement of going backstage after an energetic dance performance was for many men subconsciously bound up with the natural body scents exuded by the dancers

▲ In parts of the world where it is acceptable to expose the more important erogenous zones, facial make-up, while important, is seen as a contributing part of the total body package and not, as in the west, a major factor

▶ Expensive, extravagant hats have always been an important factor in power dressing

and the head of a black raven as a hair dye. According to Aristophanes, Athenian women used mascara made from antimony ore, white lead as face powder, an eye shadow made from seaweed extracts, red dye on their lips and grease paints of varying colours prepared from rendered down sweat obtained from Athenian sheep, mixed with human saliva and pulverized excrement of Egyptian crocodiles. A far cry from Helena Rubenstein, yet many of today's ingredients are very similar in origin.

Women who used cosmetics, perfumes and other beauty aids during Greek and Roman times had their critics and detractors, which in many ways proves that these artificial pigments and powders actually have the desired effect: they do make the human body sexier and more attractive — and they do create a great deal of attention.

It is also an undeniable fact that the human body undergoes physiological changes when sexually aroused, and the real appeal of such aids as perfume and cosmetics is that they mimic these changes. Eyes glisten, the pupils dilate and the eyelids become more colourful. Lips redden, cheeks and earlobes blush. And all of this can be achieved with cosmetics. As the author Rémy de Gourmont hypothesised earlier this century "the idea of feminine beauty is not an unmixed idea, it is intimately united with the idea of carnal pleasure." And as our history shows, there are women who will stop at nothing in their quest to fulfil their sexual potential.

PERFUME

Havelock Ellis draws attention to the ancient oriental use of perfumes and their aphrodisiacal qualities. "In the *Arabian Nights*", he states "there are many allusions to the use of

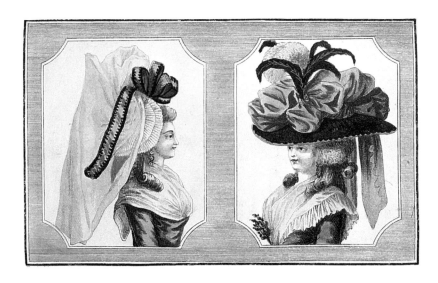

perfumes by women with a more-or-less definitely stated aphrodisiacal intent. Thus we read in the story of Kamaralzaman: With fine incense I will perfume my breasts, my belly, my whole body, so that my skin may melt more sweetly in thy mouth . . ." And he says the Islamic book, *The Perfumed Garden* by Sheik Nefzaoui, shows that in the East, "the use of perfumes by women, as well as by men, excites to the generative act", concluding that: "It is largely in reliance on this fact that in many parts of the world, especially among Eastern people and occasionally among ourselves in Europe, women have been accustomed to perfume the body and especially the vulva."

Interestingly enough, Ellis also quotes a number of women who he had interviewed whilst writing his *Studies* during the late Victorian period who were well aware of the effects of some perfumes and who experienced "a considerable degree of pleasurable sexual excitement . . . even to the extent of the moistening of the pudenda" which he concluded was "reasonable proof of the close connection between the sense of smell and the sexual organs." He also wrote at length of the special scent of musk and of various flowers, referring in particular to the lily which he said many of the ladies interviewed had described as particularly sexual "although these persons were quite unaware that Hindu authors long since described the vulva after coitus, as perfumed like the lily that has newly burst."

During the 16th to the 18th centuries many fashionable men of great wealth and social standing also wore a considerable amount of cosmetics and perfume. This did not however indicate effeminacy, on the contrary it was a sign of leisure, rank and privilege, and many a perfumed gentleman was renowned for his consistent sexual feats.

Dr Robert Brain in *The Decorated Body (1979)* draws attention to the work of Seneca when writing of Thaïs: "Cunningly wishing to exchange her disagreeable odour for some other, she, laying aside her garments to enter the bath, cakes herself green with a depilatory or conceals herself beneath a daubing of chalk in acid or covers herself with three or four layers of rich bean unguent. When by a thousand artifices she thinks she has succeeded in making herself safe, Thaïs still smells of Thaïs".

Interestingly enough, this reference to still smelling of oneself is still a major point of contention amongst women in the west who spend billions of dollars each year on deodorants in an

▲ Around 1910 narrow-hemmed dresses became fashionable. They were almost impossible to walk in and required a hobble strap — a pair of garters linked by a short length of elastic — to be worn just above the knees to prevent the wearer from taking long strides

▲ Frills and stocking tops Hollywood style — on the set of a Busby Berkeley film

▲ *The transformation scene — a model prepares for a photographic session, and with the aid of wigs and cosmetics she becomes someone else entirely*

▲ *Modern 'bondage' gear has its origins in the styles of dress worn in 19th century bordellos, which offered a wide variety of sexual delights to both male and female customers*

attempt to remove all trace of their natural body scent, and then many more billions of dollars to replace it with a new scent. Advertisers have encouraged us to cover up our personal body odours with anti-perspirants, deodorants and synthetic aromas. But many anthropologists have noted that natural body pheromones — a natural aphrodisiac produced by our apocrine sweat glands that are located on our lips, eyelids, ears, chest, armpits and around our genital region — are much more arousing, stirring ancient memories more deeply than either sight or sound.

There is a basic biological reason for this. While our other senses relay their signals to the emotional centre of the brain via an indirect route, the nose is directly wired to this emotion centre which is deep inside the brain's primeval core. This inner region is responsible for generating our most intimate feelings, so when we meet someone that we are instantly attracted to, someone who makes our blood race and fills us with amorous desire, the cause may well be the odour molecules secreted by the body which act like love-potions.

But, try as they might, the multi-national cosmetic companies have as yet been unable to harness this natural secretion which underlies so much of our sexual attractiveness. So, instead they persuade us to eradicate our own scent. We are told "Things happen after a Badedas Bath"; "Try the Intimate Experience — Intimate, the warm loving fragrance by Revlon"; "Stayfresh — stays on all day. Stays on all night"; "The new surprising way to use Charlie perfume — its pure sex efficiency"; "The new heady fragrance by *Desire* — it loves you all over". The publicity photograph shows a beautiful woman being amorously devoured by an attractive man. The primary message is the product but the undoubted secondary message is to sell the idea of a heady and uncontrollable sexual experience.

BLACK LEATHER AND CHAINS

Unfortunately our current concepts of clothing and self-presentation are imprisoned by the phenomenon of commercialized fashion, and what we wear rarely celebrates an aesthetic statement of form and colour aimed at adorning, rather than merely covering the body. What we celebrate is our conformity rather than our individuality.

▶ *Wearing only Chanel No. 5, Marilyn Monroe's career took off after the publication of this calendar, and so did the sales of Chanel perfume, thanks to Marilyn's chance remark to a reporter*

BONDAGE

In the past people thought quite differently about their bodies and their methods of displaying them. If they were wealthy enough and powerful enough they utilized an astounding melange of dress styles, many of them designed specifically to restrict the wearer's movements. For our ancestors this appears to have been an important ingredient in their mode of self presentation.

If we examine the modes of dress that have been fashionable since the end of the Middle Ages we find that some form of physical restriction, or constriction, appears to have been a necessary ingredient before the mode gained wide social acceptance: a hem of a skirt so tight it was almost impossible to walk; a man's suit cut in such a way that it was impossible for him to carry out any form of manual task; a wig so tall and cumbersome that it was difficult to move the head; a skirt so wide that it prevented the wearer from passing through a doorway unaided; a waistline so tight that it deformed the ribcage; trousers so closely fitting that the wearer was prevented from sitting down; an ornate neck ruff which rendered eating impossible; or sleeves which inconveniently covered the hands, and cumbersome bustles, high tight necklines, high-heeled shoes, tight figure-hugging skirts and really tight-fitting jeans.

These styles made the wearers very conscious of their bodies, as explained by Hermann Lotze in his theory concerning the *Extension of the Bodily Self*. This heightened body consciousness was an important ingredient in all of our ancestors' modes of dress as they were not covering their bodies out of shame or modesty. On the contrary they were using their clothing styles to project an idea of themselves in a way which they perceived was both decorative and attractive. These clothes were extensions of themselves — their top layer of skin so to speak — and under these clothes were their naked bodies. Not bodies wrapped in underclothing as is the generally accepted norm today, but naked bodies which could often be glimpsed during movement, when sitting, or when going up a flight of stairs.

HEIGHTENED BODY AWARENESS

Many women's fashions prior to the 19th century also reflected their love of coquetry and artifice together with a touch of the fetishistic, which they used to stimulate the interest of the opposite sex. This is why these styles seem so strange

▲ Heightened prestige and body awareness were the enjoyable side-effects of cumbersome styles such as the crinoline

▲ Many generations ago, lovers wrote with considerable passion about 'The Girdle of Venus', the name given to the chastity belt, and other such devices made of steel and leather that were used by both sexes to heighten the anticipation and pleasure of love

▶▶ The average naked human body is not very aesthetically pleasing or erotically exciting, as most visitors to a nudist camp would readily confirm. The appeal of serious bondage gear would appear to lie in a partly-clad body redolent with erotic symbolism. The 'bondage look' has entered the realms of both street fashion and haute couture

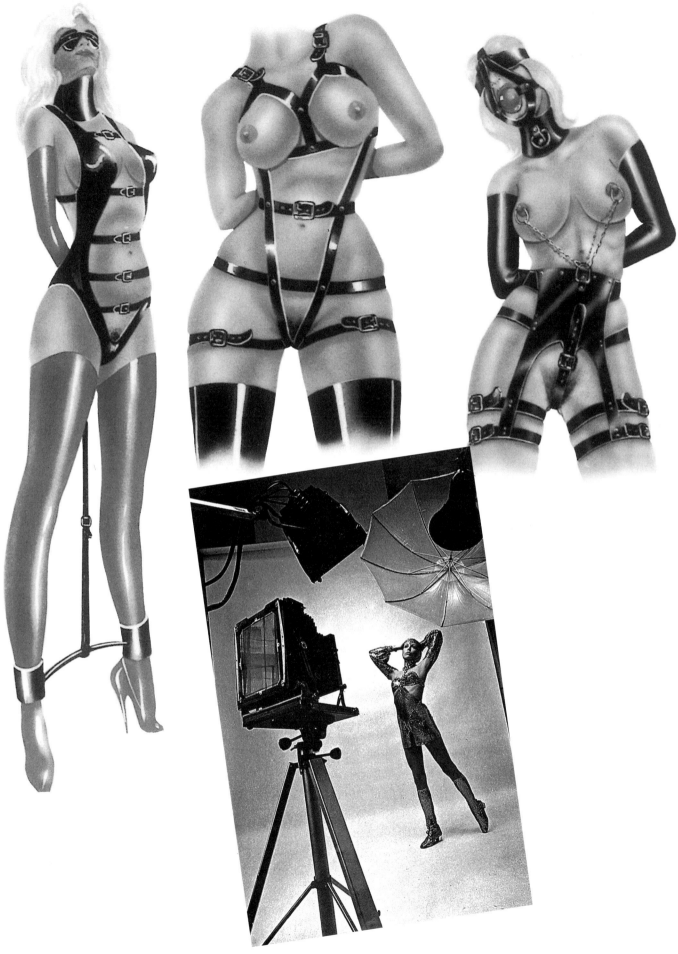

to our eyes and why we find it hard to believe that women really wore such cumbersome and restrictive styles. But then we tend to look at them in the same way as we look at our own garments, and try to imagine ourselves living our current way of life dressed in these curious yet provocative styles. It would be better to consider these fashions in the same genre as the fantasy clothing of today that many people who are rich and randy still enjoy wearing to fullfil their sexual fantasies. The only difference being that in the past the rich and powerful had no need to hide their lusty desires, whereas today such styles are not often displayed although they are much more widely worn in the privacy of wealthy homes than is commonly supposed.

VICTORIAN PRUDERY

The mid-to-late 19th century fashions, and indeed many of the early 20th century fashions worn by both men and women, were just as restrictive as many of the earlier high-fashion styles, and they too must have made the wearers very conscious of their bodies, which could not fail to arouse their sexual ardour. But during this period social attitudes toward sex and sensuality appear to have been very much of the 'close your eyes and think of England' variety, and therefore I must conclude that in some way or other people must have found sexual pleasure in this very repressiveness, in much the same way that many sexual deviants today find frissons of pleasure in self denial.

The really rich members of society, however, were not caught-up in this melange of sexual suppression and deviation, preferring to live by the social standards of their rich forebears. They created a world inhabited by the *demi-mondaines* who knew all the arts of love and pleasure, whilst the rich wives and society hostesses indulged in numerous clandestine affairs. And they too discovered that restrictive and all-concealing modes of attire, together with artifice and coquetry, greatly increased their own sexual pleasures by increasing the ardour of their lovers.

▲▲▲ *The Victorians were a funny lot. Their extraordinarily restrictive fashions became such an essential part of their psyche that they even wore them when climbing the Alps. Well-off women also went to meetings to decide what the working classes should wear and they condemned female mine workers as whores and harlots for wearing trousers as they delineated the legs*

We exclaim 'what a beautiful little foot!' when we have merely seen a pretty shoe. We admire a lovely waist when nothing has met our eyes but an elegant girdle.

Goethe

▲ *Morals in the 19th century fluctuated widely. On the one hand were the virtuous and morally-indignant middle-classes, and at the other were scenes of total debauchery and abandonment. High society figures were regular visitors to the Dance Theatres and Music Halls of London, Paris and New York, which regularly featured explicit nudity and, according to some accounts, bestiality*

Here and Now

*B*y 1950 fashion had at last become democratic. From then on the newest styles became available to anyone who had a few dollars to spend on the way they looked. Those who were prepared to spend the most were the unattached females who were actively looking for a mate. This dramatic change gave birth to a new kind of fashion industry; an industry which over the next decade was going to revolutionize not only the way people looked but also the way they thought about clothes. Designers were now free to create new forms of clothing specifically aimed at the young, nubile members of society.

▲▲▶ *The mass media was quick to detect the thirst for glamour after the war years. Striking styles for the 'younger generation' became headline news, although many older men continued to wear a traditional suit for most occasions. Bold new styles such as those worn by stars such as Elvis Presley and Brigitte Bardot had immense appeal for the young, but confused and angered many of the older generation who often accused the young of undermining the very foundations of democratic society*

FASHION SINCE THE FIFTIES

The early years of the 1950s were a period of great change. The Second World War had extracted a heavy toll, tens of millions had died and few had escaped being touched by misery and hardship. Recovery was slow, and armed conflict still dominated the world political scene. The values of the pre-war years were gone forever.

THE GLOBAL VILLAGE

Television had been introduced into many thousands of homes, bringing evidence of change from around the world into the

living-rooms of ordinary families, and the cinema was changing to meet the challenge of this new form of mass communication. Marlon Brando had become a big star with such films as *The Wild One* and *On the Waterfront*, and the rebellious image he portrayed echoed the mood of the younger generation. Marilyn Monroe was greatly admired for her unfettered, vulnerable, magnetic allure. She too was helping to break down the outdated, puritan moral ethic of the older generation who were still trying to recreate a society based on 1930s values.

The young actresses Audrey Hepburn and Leslie Caron were admired by the younger generation for their waifish looks. The pundits declared they had "so captured the young imagination, and the mood of our time, that they have established a new kind of beauty — a beauty which many girls are now copying." The following year another movie star was going to add her influence to the way young girls were going to look. Her name was Brigitte Bardot and the film was *And God created Woman*, directed by Roger Vadim. Soon B.B's nubile charms were seen in every newspaper and magazine, outraging the older generation and shocking the ecclesiastics. Her shimmering promiscuity and wayward looks were exactly in tune with the new young generation.

▲ ▲ *The blow-up bra helped many an image-conscious girl achieve the popular Jane Russell silhouette of the 1950s*

HARLOTS, WHORES AND WILD ANIMALS

Chuck Berry, Bill Haley and the Comets, Little Richard and Fats Domino had begun to change the popular music scene with songs like *Shake, Rattle and Roll*, *Rock Around the Clock* and *Sweet Little Sixteen*. Elvis Presley had just started his professional career and within months his records were topping the music charts and his films were playing to capacity audiences of young devotees everywhere. His audiences copied

◀ ▲▲ *In the more traditional areas of fashion, women avidly followed the progress of the new French designers. They dreamt of owning a seductive ball gown by Balenciaga, Jacques Fath or Dior, whose flattering A, Y, Tulip and Sack lines were particularly popular. Traditional forms of menswear also began to adjust to the more fashion-conscious times and a distinct Edwardian influence emerged amongst the young city gents*

his style of casual dress — jeans, denim jacket, shirt without a tie — and moved their bodies in imitation of his. Consequently Elvis was accused of corrupting the young, encouraging hooliganism, causing young girls to behave like whores and harlots and turning nice young men into wild animals.

Headlines proclaimed: "Unless this messenger of Satan and his nigger-man music is stopped, there will be another Civil War." The schism between the old and young generations was now almost complete.

The new generation of the mid-to-late 1950s was affluent. They were restless for change and they were jaded by the years of shortages. They were tired of being criticized. They wanted their own leaders so that they could create their own kind of world. Politics turned them off. Hearth and home had become a joke. Ambition, hard work, and dedication to duty had done nothing for their parents' generation but leave them sucked dry. What they wanted was to have fun, to enjoy the sort of music they liked and to exploit their own particular physical charms in new styles of clothing which would give them a common identity.

I was an art student in London at the time and I saw at first hand the changes going on around me. The young female students were making short, tight skirts which emphasized the roundness of their bottoms and displayed their knees and often the upper part of their thighs. Tights had not yet become widely available, so these students wore their proto-type minis with black stockings and suspenders. And when they sat down, or climbed up a flight of stairs, a pink flash of thigh was occasionally 'accidentally' visible. Some of the more shapely female students also wore tight sweaters which displayed their *Spirilla*-shaped breasts, and they tightened their wide patent leather belts to display a narrow waistline — all of which emphasized their nubility and clearly distinguished them from their mothers' generation.

The young males of that period were also easily distinguishable from their fathers' generation, having discarded the obligatory dark suit, collar and tie. They wore their longer hair, winklepicker shoes, waisted jackets, narrow trousers without turn-ups, coloured shirts and narrow ties. They looked like Edwardian Dandies. Some were wearing proto-type Teddy-boy styles, characterized by their brothel-creeper, crepe-soled shoes and long, square-cut jackets with velvet collar and cuffs. Others had adopted Elvis-style jeans, casual shirts and denim jackets. And yet another faction adopted leather motorcycle

▲ *In 1953 Marlon Brando starred in* The Wild One, *followed in 1954 by* On The Waterfront. *In 1955, the James Dean films* Rebel Without a Cause *and* East of Eden *were released, and in 1956 Elvis Presley appeared on the screens in* Love Me Tender. *In 1957* Jailhouse Rock *and* Loving You *were playing to packed houses. Men's fashion would never be the same again*

▲ *Television helped to spread the popularity of the new 50s fashions.* The Six Five Special, *avidly watched by the fashion-conscious younger generation, quickly became a hit show. Like the many music and youth culture shows that were to follow, it asserted the dynamism of the new generation and established the fact that the young had a style of their own*

▲ *André Courréges, leader of a new group of young Paris designers, caused a sensation with his collection of 1966*

▲ *The psychedelic designs of New York's Oscar de la Renta made for vivid fashion pages in 1967*

jackets, form-fitting trousers, T-shirts and heavy military-style boots, a style made famous by Brando in *On the Waterfront* and later to become associated with the Hell's Angels.

HAUTE COUTURE LOSES ITS GRIP

Establishment fashions were also beginning to change. Many of the great couture houses of the 1930s and 40s were now reduced to labels on bottles of perfume. Chanel, Molyneux, Piquet, Lelong, Schiaparelli, Rochas and Jacques Fath had all closed down in the early 1950s, although both Chanel and Molyneux were soon to re-open to boost the lagging sales of their perfumes. The two great names in Paris in the mid-1950s were Christian Dior and Cristobal Balenciaga. They were great because they were receptive to change. They employed untried young designers who were destined to become the fashion leaders of the mid-1960s: Dior recruited the talented 19-year-old Yves Saint Laurent, and Balenciaga hired the revolutionary André Courrèges.

In the spring of 1958 Yves Saint Laurent's first collection for the House of Dior was shown — Christian Dior having died of a heart attack several months earlier. The St Laurent

▲ *In the mid 60s the California based designer Rudi Gernreich made headline news with his topless bathing suit*

▲ *Work by the Japanese designer Issey Mayake did much to break old moulds and make unisex styles more acceptable*

▲ *Castillo's tarty look — sold in the Left Bank boutiques of Paris in 1968*

collection was a great success, he was hailed as "the saviour of France" and the press declared that "the great Dior tradition will continue!" But the following autumn Paris fashion was in turmoil as St Laurent let his young ideas flow. He had dared to bare the knees of respectable women and was accused of making them look like "Left Bank Hippies". A British M.P. announced: "I think it is ridiculous for a young man of 23 to try to dictate to sensible women. British women will not take any notice of this nonsense!" In America, *A Little Below the Knee Clubs* were quickly formed to try and prevent such a dramatic change.

The new fashion had arrived. Skirts were shorter because the younger generation wished to show their knees and by sheer weight of numbers and spending power they had taken over the fashion scene. This was the heyday of the 'baby boomers'. Never before had there been such a high percentage of teenagers in the population of western Europe, and they were making their presence felt.

Fashion pundits everywhere were outraged that the young Yves St Laurent was attempting to change the direction of fashion single-handedly and demanded his sacking. With the

> *A fashion ceases to be fashionable the moment the masses at large are wearing it.*
> Christian Dior *1955*

> *Fashion is in the air borne upon the wind. One intuits it. It comes from new inventions, manners, events; and it affects all things.*
> Gabrielle Chanel

Fashion pundits of the 60s avidly sought sensational new designs that would make headline news. See-through clothing by Paris based designer Louis Feraud was a great success as were Mary Quant's wacky designs

benefit of hindsight we can see that St Laurent was simply and accurately reflecting the changes that were inevitable as the younger generation began exerting its influence. But nevertheless he was removed from his position as chief designer at the House of Dior and replaced by the more traditionally-minded Marc Bohan. By repressing young fashion, Paris remained for the time being, the centre of the established mode, and the new collections were dutifully recorded in the prestigious glossy magazines of the period.

Regardless of all the mass-media hype for haute couture, a revolution had begun in the ready-to-wear industry — taking it into new territories and making bigger profits than ever before. For the first time ever, fashion was being created by the working classes and was assuming a universal importance that was making headlines everywhere. Fashion was destined never to be the same again.

In the early 1960s, the Paris couture houses continued to produce desirable, wearable clothes aimed at the middle-class market. The press, whilst dutifully supporting these collections, was nevertheless a-twitter with rumours that many couturiers were considering abandoning haute couture altogether to concentrate on the more profitable ready-to-wear industry. St Laurent re-emerged in 1962 to open his own small *salon* financed by $50,000 he had received from the House of Dior as settlement for breach of contract, and his *Rive Gauche* ready-to-wear designs were soon selling world wide. But by then the centre of young fashion had moved to London's Carnaby Street and King's Road where the dress boutiques run by designers like Mary Quant, Tuffin and Foale, James Wedge at Countdown, Barbara Hulanicki at Biba, and Ossie Clark at Quorum had out-dated Paris couture; and they were to dominate the fashion scene throughout the 1960s and into the early 1970s.

THE SWINGING SIXTIES

The new jet-paced world was impatient for change and novelty, and this was better supplied by the young innovative designers of London and the boutique designers of New York and Paris, than by the world of haute couture. There were some notable exceptions, however: Courrèges' revolutionary trouser and mini suit designs of 1964; Paco Rabane's metal and plastic designs of 1966; the Space Age designs of Emmanuel Ungaro and Yves St Laurent's 1968 see-through dresses.

In London there were dozens of new young designers

emerging from art schools, bursting with new ideas and pushing the frontiers of change forward. British *Vogue* proclaimed: "For the first time the young people who work in the rag-trade are making and promoting the clothes they naturally like, clothes which are relevant to the way they live . . . ours is the first generation that can express itself on its own terms."

UNISEX

The young males and females of the late 1960s and early 1970s did not want to look as if they belonged to separate species — they had seen the trouble caused in their parents' generation. They wanted to be friends and to share their future together. They didn't subscribe to the dominant husband and submissive wife syndrome. They enjoyed each other's company, they felt equal and, thanks to the sexual revolution and the pill, they didn't need to dress to express their sexual identity all the time. In fact, it became part of the fashion to dress in a similar manner for some of the time, so that when they changed into their male or female styles the difference would have more impact.

The young people themselves had no difficulty telling male from female, even though the older generation claimed

▲ *In her films in the 50s the French actress Brigitte Bardot was presented in anything from nothing to grand evening dress but was most often seen clad in traditionally erotic garments such as stockings & suspenders or metal-studded black leather*

◀ *Publicly abandoning items of clothing became quite a trend in the 60s and 70s. Whether it be stripping off at a rock concert or a ritual bra burning, a political statement was consciously or unconsciously being made and such acts were widely reported*

> *The society which produces changing fashions must itself be a society which is changing.*
> Prof. Quentin Bell *1947*

confusion. The sexually aware had learnt to read the differences between the crotch-bulge of the male and the crotch-gap of the female. They could also tell at a glance the bum shapes of the sexes, the distinctive sway of the back, the differences in the mode of walking and standing — even when sitting the physical differences caused little confusion.

THE RULES OF THE GAME

The hype and the anger over these new fashions were only to be expected. The young generation had simply selected a mode of dressing which utilized a new angle on an old ploy — a variation on the sex attraction game which attempts to exclude all of those who do not know the rules. Those who don't know the rules get angry. It's a ploy which has continued up until the present day: each new generation has invented its own set of rules of sexual display in order to set itself apart, and each of these styles has been met with an antagonistic attack by members of the older generation.

POLITICAL DRESSING

The use of dress as a means of expressing a political opinion is not new, particularly in male attire which by tradition is usually influenced more by economic, industrial and political factors than by the vagaries of fashion.

REVOLUTIONARY CHIC

The most notable example of 'political dressing' was during the French Revolution when the fashionable styles worn at the court of Versailles immediately categorized the wearer as a Royalist and therefore liable to instant arrest or lynching.

Another example can be found earlier in the 18th century, when the radical English Whigs were aiming to subordinate the British monarchy to the control of Parliament. The Whigs wore a distinctive facial patch on the left hand side of their faces, whilst the Tories, who supported the king and the inherited status-quo, sported a facial patch on the right. This is the origin of the use of the words left and right to define political beliefs. During the English Civil War the followers of republican Oliver Cromwell threw away their lace trimmings and silken frills, cut off their curls and became known as Roundheads. Their royalist opponents, the Cavaliers, were distinguished by their long flowing locks and their expensive and flamboyant clothes which, needless to say, went swiftly to the back of the wardrobe the moment they were defeated.

▲▲ New working class modes of dress originated in the mid-to-late 1950s as the younger members of the British work force struggled to free themselves from inherited prejudices. They demanded the right to be dressed in styles that reflected their new attitudes and way of life. This period saw the emergence of distinctively dressed groups: Teddy Boys in their drapes and brothel-creepers; Hell's Angels, whose quasi-uniform of militarised black leather was worn by male and female alike; and their antithesis the sharply dressed Mods. Such visual differences distinguished one group from another as well as setting all apart from the older generation

CND CHIC

By the beginning of the 19th century it was clearly established that any form of flamboyance in men's dress was distinctly anti-democratic, and therefore to be regarded with great suspicion. A business suit and a short haircut became an almost obligatory uniform for men, and was to remain virtually unchallenged until the mid-to-late 1950s when the ban-the-bomb protesters united in their efforts to stop the spread of nuclear weapons. Many of these protesters were, in fact, the leading intellectuals of the day who, by chance, cared less for their appearance than their contemporaries. They did not wear the customary suit, nor were they accustomed to having their hair cut regularly. They also wore a distinctive badge on their lapel, a symbol of the Campaign for Nuclear Disarmament, and refused to be cowed by threats from police or politicians. Soon long hair, scruffy clothing and ban-the-bomb badges became, by association, a defiant symbol of political dissent, making the wearer liable to summary arrest on the slightest provocation.

▲▼ *In the 1960s the questioning intellectuals, together with the younger members of society, took on the forces of the law in their battle for freedom of choice — regarding both clothing and lifestyle*

WORKING CLASS CHIC

The first half of the 1950s had seen post-war austerity and deprivation greatly relaxed. For the first time in over 15 years and, arguably, the first time ever for the working class, teenage males had money to spare and the necessary leisure time in which to experiment with the colour, shape and style of their clothing. Within five years the working class males had become the new arbiters of style, and they let it be known that they were no longer willing to follow the dictates of those in authority or the stultifying influence of tradition.

Their non-conformity met with a full-scale establishment attack on the Teddy Boy fashions of the late 1950s. The Teddy Boys styled their hair in imitation of Elvis, their hero, and wore their hair longer than usual to signal that they were civilians, not short-haired army conscripts serving a compulsory stretch of National Service.

The Teddy Boys' distinctive clothing was aimed at emphasizing the wearer's open sexuality, bravado and toughness. Their behaviour often bordered on the violent as if to demonstrate that although they were dressed differently from other males they were not effeminate — a very important distinction for all working-class males.

The Mods (short for modernists) became a fashion force in the early 1960s, at the same time as Adam Faith, the Small Faces, Herman's Hermits and the early days of London's Carnaby Street. Again it was a style-conscious working class mode. Mods wore narrow lapels, a narrow tie, narrow cuffless trousers and narrow pointed shoes. They were the antithesis of the Hell's Angels who rode motor cycles and wore heavy leather metal-studded jackets — the first anti-fashion style, intended to shock rather than please.

▼ *The ever-diminishing miniskirt of the 60s turned heads and raised eyebrows. For the wearer it was a powerful expression of freedom and sexual independence*

▼ *Although neat and tidy by today's standards, The Beatles were attacked in the early 60s for their long hair and unconventional dress. When, in 1965, they were awarded the MBE for their services to popular music many members of the establishment returned their awards to Buckingham Palace in protest*

▲ *The campaign for world peace gained great support in the 1960s. Flower Power not military power was the cry of the young, and their casual hand-knits and jeans were a non-verbal statement of their politics*

▼ *Student protests against armed conflict and repression became increasingly strident in the 1960s. Confrontations took place on American college campuses as early as 1962, and in Indonesia student riots had become almost commonplace by the mid 60s. The culmination came in 1968 with the Paris riots which were so violent that it seemed the younger generation had irrevocably renounced all the imposed rules of established authority. With this outburst, clothing as a means of self expression finally came of age*

Next came the Skinheads, who became a symbol of working class right-wing political dissent, clearly different from their arch-rivals, the long-haired, basically middle class, left-wing Flower People.

CORPORATE CHIC

In opposition to this swelling tide, the established Corporate Man expressed his faith in the existing order by having his hair cut in the regulation 'short back and sides', and by wearing a very conservative dark suit with a white shirt and old school or plain-coloured tie. His wife dressed in an inconspicuous style, preferring a cashmere twin set and pleated tweed skirt to anything remotely 'fashionable'. In fact 'fashion' had become almost a dirty word amongst established executives and their families, and their anti-fashion stance was aimed at visibly separating the wealthy executives from the newly fashionable working class.

DROP-OUT CHIC

The beatniks were creating headline news in the early-to-mid 1960s as settlement after settlement of young people — described in the establishment press as "anti-social hoodlums who believe in free love and anarchy" — was formed. The beatniks deliberately chose a shabby mode of attire, purchased from Army Surplus Stores or at second-hand clothing exchanges. They wore dark glasses as a badge of identification and they lived in communal groups, squatting in disused factories and derelict houses. Their numbers grew enormously in the mid-60s with an influx of college students who joined the beatnik groups as a social protest. Many of the males grew beards and sported long hair as a symbol of their growing disenchantment with the increasingly materialistic, industrialized world and what they perceived as society's uncaring attitude towards minority groups.

URBAN GUERILLA CHIC

The practice of wearing surplus military garments as a pseudo-urban guerrilla uniform grew out of beatnik anti-fashion statements. The uniform was worn by young people who wished to show their sympathy for freedom-fighters who were creating riots and open warfare in many parts of the world. The increasing use of denim clothing by college students had also developed political significance, which came to the fore during the college strikes, sit-ins and riots against the Vietnam

▲ In the 1970s photographs of urban guerillas often appeared in the press, many showing young girls — victims of a totalitarian regime — in proletarian styles of dress. Such pictures added fuel to the fire of those in the west struggling for equal rights and freedom of self-expression

▲ Creative dressing is a powerful means of individual expression and is often the first right to be denied by a repressive government

war and the army draft which erupted spontaneously throughout the western world between 1965 and 1968.

1968 was the year of the student riots in Paris. In the very birthplace of haute couture, clothes had become a means of expressing one's political beliefs rather than an allegiance to one couture house or another. If all the *contestataires* who rioted and marched, built and defended the street barricades that year, looked alike in jeans and sweaters, worn with scarves to protect their faces against the effects of tear gas, it was because they wanted to tell each other who they were and which side they were on. Axel Madsen described the situation: "Jeans were not only clothes; they were clothes-language, instant and eloquent symbols of brotherhood; unity-in-protest clothes that talked body language."

Other political and moral beliefs were also being expressed as women discarded their bras and girdles, a symbol to them of female repression. Streaking became commonplace and nude bathing made an appearance. In fact, not since the early days of the French Revolution had so much change taken place in the western mode of dress, and not since the English Civil War had so much sartorial symbolism been used to signal the wearer's political and moral beliefs.

CLOTHES FOR THE PROLES

Realising that clothing is a form of self-expression, some governments have, at various times, attempted to control all clothing styles. They wanted to control the people's hearts and minds, so they started with their exterior symbols — their garments. They decreed that these garments conform to certain moral and social standards, that they were comfortable and easy to work in, practical and unadorned and that they cover areas of the wearer's anatomy that they thought people may find offensive. Political control of clothing has been attempted in China, in Cuba and in certain Eastern bloc countries, with the result that the very items of clothing themselves, far from becoming symbols of solidarity and the joy of working for the common good, become highly visible symbols of repression. Drab and bleak and anonymous, such garments deny man's essential 'humanness' — denying an individual's right to free expression in exactly the same way as a prison uniform.

20TH CENTURY INFLUENCES

At a very early age, even before they can properly communicate with other people, children learn from storybooks about the magical power of dress. They yearn to look like the illustrations of Prince Charming or Snow White, to have hair like Rapunzel or small feet like Cinderella. This desire to match reality with an image does not stop with fairy tales.

POP STARS

As children grow, their heroes and heroines change, and since the 1950s each succeeding generation has imitated its favourite pop and rock stars. The intervening years have seen clones of Elvis Presley, Blondie, The Tubes, Queen, Tina Turner, Kiss, Adam Ant, Prince, Cher, Toyah Wilcox, Boy George, Kate Bush, The Beatles, Madonna and many many more. Many

Pop and the new young fashions are closely linked. Singers have taken over from society hostesses and top models as the taste setters of our time.
Fashion editorial, 1976

▲ Traditionally children have learnt about the magical powers of dress through illustrations in story books and dreamt of wearing fairytale outfits, but the 1950s saw a change. From this time onwards children began to fantasise about looking like their new idols — pop singers, and members of dance teams

▲▲▲ For children in the 70s identification with a pop group had priority over flattering individual body shape. Kiss, The Beatles, The Bay City Rollers, Blondie, and The Sex Pistols have all had their influence for better or worse

of the recent trends for skimpy black leather outfits trimmed with metal studs and chains, or those made from sequins with fur and feather trimmings, cut-off tank-tops, and an assortment of bondage and fetish-style garments can be directly traced back to the stage costumes worn by the tyros of modern music. That the young desire to copy these fashions is as inevitable and understandable as the urge their parents or grandparents felt to look like Joan Crawford, Ginger Rogers, James Dean, Loretta Young, one of the Goldwyn Girls, Robert Redford, Marlon Brando or any other Hollywood star, all of whom greatly influenced the fashions and morals of their day.

GIRLIE MAGAZINES

Strippers and show girls whose photographs appear in *Men Only*, *Club International*, *Penthouse* and *Playboy*, have been exciting young males ever since the relaxation of the censorship laws in the early 1960s. In their turn, many young females have been inspired to be somewhat more daring in their erotic displays, and several of their pop and rock star heroes have featured as barely-clad centerfolds — Prince and Madonna for instance. But then similar displays of seductive charm were also published in their parents' and grandparents' day. Joan Crawford and Jean Harlow were splashed over magazines minimally clad in the late 1920s, Lana Turner in the 1930s, Jane Russell in the 1940s and, of course, Marilyn Monroe in the 1950s.

TELEVISION

Today's young people have also been exposed to sexy television advertisements inspired by *Penthouse* style nudity and aimed at selling anything from sports cars to health food. They will have watched many travelogue programs about exotic locations and exotic peoples, and the cathode ray tube will have beamed them into the heart of the famous carnivals of Rio De Janeiro, New Orleans and Venice where both men and women dress up and decorate themselves in the most exotic ways and cross-dressing is almost commonplace. They will have seen light entertainment programs from Caesar's Palace in Las Vegas and the Lido in Paris featuring lines of near-naked, high-kicking girls, and boys dressed up as girls. And they will have been influenced by televised dance groups like *Hot Gossip*, featuring both male and female dancers in exotic and erotic costumes, which enlivened many British television shows in the late 1970s and early 80s.

▲▲▲ *Magazines like Mayfair, and films like* Emmanuelle *have helped make the display of erogenous zones and dressing up for sex more acceptable*

SPORT

Sporting personalities have also contributed to the montage of sartorial styles from which the current young generation can now choose. Who could have failed to appreciate the visual impact of Olga Korbut or Nadia Comaneci in the early 1970s and their contribution to the '*Let's Get Physical*' fashions for skimpy leotards and bare thighs that are still so popular? The current craze for aerobic exercise has kept the leotard market in business as well as having an effect on how people perceive their bodies. Aerobics heralded the era of keeping fit, exercising and jogging — all of which required new forms of apparel.

[Bottom] '*Gorgeous Gussie's* frilly panties caused quite a stir when they appeared on Wimbledon's centre court in 1949. Although just as concealing as the regulation plain white knickers, the lace frills were interpreted as a provocative form of sexual display

▼ The shoulder and thigh padding of the American football player clearly exaggerates the masculine form to almost superhuman proportions and creates an impression of enormous physical power

▲ If the fertility rites of Amazon Indians could be shown on TV in the west, who could blame the young viewers who wished to be similarly adorned for the local summer dance?

▶ Nubile cheer-leaders flaunt their physical charms to enhance the masculinity of the players and gain the support of the crowd

▲ Television coverage of festivals, carnivals and mardi gras around the globe as well as the screening of Las Vegas strip shows opened the eyes of the public to imaginative and erotic styles of dressing

Jogging gear became normal casual wear for many people, in fact track suits and running shoes can be seen on the shelves of supermarkets up and down the country and they are worn by young and old alike, whether or not they partake in any form of physical exertion.

The snob element of expensive sports such as golf, horse-riding, polo, car rallying and yachting has also had an effect on current styles. With more leisure time and an increase in spending power, more people began to partake in these sports, purchasing the necessary items of apparel which they wore for non-sporting activities as a symbol of their new-found wealth and leisure. It became fashionable, for instance, to wear some forms of après-ski clothing whilst visiting friends in the country at weekends as this was a display of both wealth and a newly-acquired skill.

ADVERTISING

The advertising industry does not produce anything to actually buy or sell or wear, but it nevertheless has an enormous effect on the way we live and dress. Wherever we live, every day,

PROTAGONISTA DONNA.

bologna & figli

▲ *Advertisements have done much to increase the public's tolerance to nudity. the female body was presented as an If aesthetic sculptural form this excused its nakedness and helped to make other forms|of nudity more acceptable*

▼ *The female belly button was a taboo display feature until the advent of the bikini, when this previously hidden erotic area suddenly became a selling point*

we see dozens of publicity images in newspapers and in magazines, on billboards and on television. No other form of imagery confronts us quite so frequently. One may remember or forget these visual messages but, briefly, one takes them in.

These images have been designed to propose to each of us that we will be able to transform ourselves, or our lives, by buying something extra. We are persuaded to look upon the models in the advertisement as people who have been transformed by this product. This in turn, so the theory goes, makes us envious, and envy is the motivation to purchase. We are also motivated in many instances to attempt to look and dress like the models we envy. Of course, in reality this is impossible. Not even the model looks like the person we see in the photograph or on the television.

How does such palpably fraudulent publicity remain credible — or credible enough to exert the influence it does? It remains credible because the images are judged, not by real fulfillment of expectations, but by the relevance of the fantasies they create in the mind of the spectator-buyer. Its essential appeal is not to reality but to day-dreaming. And it is this day-dreaming which gradually opens the door to change. Without it we would still be as inhibited about our modes of dress as they were in Victorian times.

Belly Button Contest

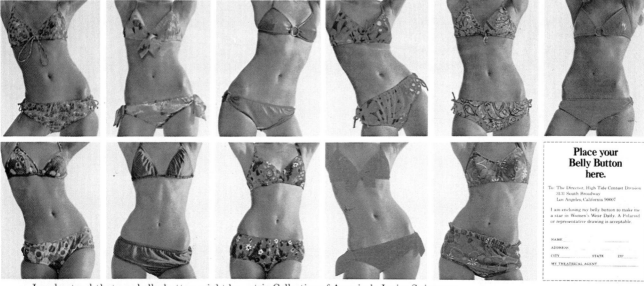

Place your Belly Button here.

To: The Director, High Tide Contest Division
3131 South Broadway
Los Angeles, California 90007

I am enclosing my belly button to make me a star in Women's Wear Daily. A Polaroid or representative drawing is acceptable.

NAME

ADDRESS

CITY   STATE   ZIP

MY THEATRICAL AGENT

I understand that my belly button might be published. I understand that all buyers' belly buttons entered will be judged on originality of content. I further understand that by contacting the showrooms and addresses below, I can have a Preview Look at the most Elec-

tric Collection of America's Junior Swimwear. And order beaches of super solids and prints in fabrics never before known to water. The High Tides. Because I remember how hot hot last Summer was.
I enclose my belly button.

High Tide

▲ In the 1930s only the wealthy could enjoy international travel and ocean liner was the stylish means of transport. Without a strict luggage allowance, women of fashion were able to travel with trunkloads of dresses to last the entire trip

▲ In the 1950s cheap international air travel brought new clothing influences as ethnic styles began to infiltrate western fashion through adventurous travellers who purchased exotic garments enroute. Similar styles had also been popularised in the 1920s by Rudolf Valentino who was often seen wearing exotic garments in his films

Thus the phoney world of advertising with its photographic tricks and illusions, helps move fashion on into new and more adventurous areas of experimentation, spreading the gospel of freedom of choice, a freedom which eventually results in a wider choice for all.

FARAWAY PLACES

World travel was once the prerogative of the extremely wealthy who had become accustomed to travelling by steamship, accompanied by innumerable trunk-loads of clothing. But when travel by airship and intercontinental aeroplanes became a reality in the late 1920s, the trunks of elaborate clothing were replaced by lightweight luggage filled with easy-to-pack travel outfits. The need for such travel clothes greatly influenced the new fashions, and those who could afford the air fares demonstrated the fact with the lightweight, non-crushable styles they wore.

With the introduction of jumbo jets, worldwide travel became a possibility for all. Soon many people were travelling to India, the Pacific Islands, South Africa, Brazil or Mexico for their holidays and, naturally, as luggage space was at a premium, people began buying their holiday clothes at their distant destinations and returning with selected items for wearing at weekends or for a party. Gradually the modes of dress which had originated in Cairo, Delhi, Bangkok or Rio became fashionable in Europe, America and Australia and large numbers of these garments were imported for sale. People became used to the texture of exotic fabrics, to unusual colours and patterns, and this influenced their choice of new western fashions.

In cities like Bangkok and Cairo, with an ever-increasing number of western tourists as potential customers, the indigenous dress manufacturers adapted their merchandise to appeal more to the western customers, improving the cut and fit to please the tourists. They also began to copy some of the western styles, which not only sold at bargain rates to their overseas customers, but also to the residents of these cities who wished to look like the tourists.

With so many tourists visiting so many countries, various influences began to mix. Design ideas which had originated in Mexico were copied in London and transported to Delhi by tourists, then copied there and sold to visitors from Canada. Thus an international style of ethnic design began to evolve featuring juxtaposed patterns and colours that had their origins everywhere and nowhere.

One of the results of this melting pot of clothing styles is that many truly ethnic styles are being lost. Traditional necklaces, bracelets, earrings, hair ornaments of all sorts, clasps, beaded aprons, pieces of leatherwork, and numerous other items — many of which have been handed down for many generations — are being sold off for the tourist dollar. Many museums around the world have also been actively collecting such pieces to such an extent that it is now estimated that there are more examples of ethnic attire and adornment residing in the west than in their countries of origin.

We cannot, nor should we, deny people's desire for change, and we must therefore accept that the ethnic modes of dress worn by people in the remoter areas of the world will inevitably change, but it would be cultural vandalism if we were to allow all that tradition to disappear without making some effort to record the remaining vestiges and to save them for posterity.

FASHION MAGAZINES AND NEWSPAPERS

Fashion news in the western world is big business with handsome profits for publishing companies who are able to provide the fashion information that their customers wish to read. This may seem an easy task for those who do not realize that publicizing new fashions is not the same as predicting the new fashionable styles, as fashion journalism exists quite separately from fashion itself. Fashion is about the changing mode of dress people choose to *wear*, whilst fashion journalism is about new modes of dress that people wish to *read about* without necessarily wishing to purchase and wear them.

The art of fashion journalism therefore is to feature the styles which will fascinate, intrigue and excite the readers so that they will buy more fashion publications. This is why, if one looks back at fashion magazines and newspaper editorials published during the past 25 years it is almost impossible to find examples of the clothes featured actually being worn by members of the public.

Modern fashion journalism, therefore, created new opportunities in fashion design, as designers realized that they needed to produce news-worthy styles that would catch the fashion journalist's eye. An appetite for news-worthiness had been noted back in the early 1930s whilst the author Eliot Hodgkin, in *Fashion Drawing* (1932), was discussing the problems involved with illustrating the latest Paris fashions: "This information reaches a public which cannot, in 99 cases out of 100, afford to buy advanced fashions from Paris and would

▲ Fashion reporters of the 1960s would scour boutiques for new designer labels. In 1967 prestigious fashion magazines were quick to notice the unisex designs of Tom Gilbey and the Carnaby Street styles of Tuffin and Foale. Even a number of my own up-market styles were widely featured

▲ Not all members of the press are pro-fashion. Some are extremely critical of change and take it upon themselves to point the moral finger. In 1957 The Catholic Times faithfully reported the condemnations of new fashions by the leading ecclesiastics of the day

◄▲▼ *Creative use of words and images
has always been an important part of good
fashion journalism. If new ideas are
reported in an interesting, eye-catching
and humourous manner then this helps
readers to understand developments taking
place and makes them more receptive to
change. The success of many of the more
outlandish styles of the 1960s can be directly
attributed to the imaginative and appealing
way in which they were presented by the
the popular press*

not wear them even if it could. For it is an unfortunate fact that the daily press, in this sphere as in all others, gets hold of just that wild ephemeral element that startles, without having the power to please. Let an ostrich feather bustle appear at a Paris dress show, or an evening gown made of Balmoral tartan, and we shall read about it in the headlines of the morning papers, and nowhere else. If we did not read about them they would cease to exist, for it is only *pour épater le bourgeois* that such things are made."

However irritating such publicity was considered in the 1930s it became a very valuable commodity in the post-war years when copies of the latest Paris fashions became widely available at all price levels; newspaper editorials on the latest fashion craze helped sell millions of dollars worth of eye-catching styles. The Paris couturier Christian Dior was the first designer to capitalize on this when his first collection of 1947, featuring *The New Look*, became headline news around the globe. Season after season until his death in October 1957, he received world-wide publicity for his *A-line, H-line, Y-line, Empire-line, Tulip-line*, the *Chemise*, the *Sack* and many other instantly fashionable lines which were all easy to report, lending themselves to serious or light-hearted journalistic treatments with catchy headlines and eye-catching illustrations.

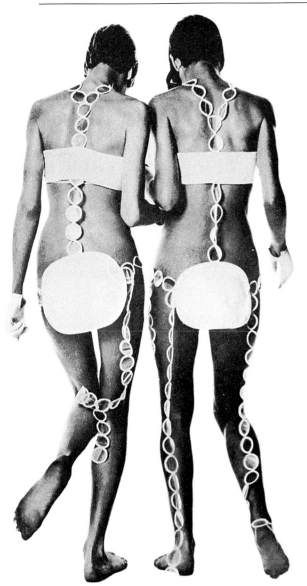

▶ ▲ *Paris designers and their advertising consultants have continued along the path of creative journalism, grabbing attention with outrageous styles*

Modesty comes and goes but common sense has always been absent and the most elementary anatomical facts have consistently been ignored.
M & A Batterberry *Mirror, Mirror, 1977*

INVENTIVE JOURNALISM

The reporters, in their search for fashion headlines which were more eye-catching than those they featured yesterday, soon found themselves caught up in the world of artificially stimulated sensationalism, and by the mid-1960s fashion reportage had evolved into a dazzling display in which many editorial presentations became as 'inventive' and 'way-out' as the styles they were featuring. If a particular fashion was not as startling as the art director wanted, then the journalist and the photographer would find ways of creating an image so that the reader would be fooled into thinking that it was.

This 'creative journalism' featured flared dresses which, with aid of pins and clips, were made to fit like a second skin, whilst green or blue filters and orange lights could change the colour and design of the fabric. If that wasn't enough to create an image to be featured under the banner headline WOULD YOU ALLOW YOUR DAUGHTER TO WEAR THIS? then the hem would be turned up to expose the top of the thigh and lengths of ribbon and braid would be added with the aid of pins and sticky-tape to draw attention to a newly-created cleavage.

The following week the fashion journalist and photographer would set to work on hot pants, thigh-length boots, see-through dresses, sexy lingerie, men's sportswear, children's clothes, leather garments, corsets or party clothes. Headlines would scream SHOW A LEG THERE, LADY! BE GLAD YOU'RE A GIRL! and DISGUSTING, BUT YOU'LL SOON BE WEARING IT!

In fact, the fashion journalists, photographers and illustrators of this period were directly responsible for popularizing many of more adventurous dress styles now being worn. Theirs was the language of change which finally wrested fashion away from the pervading influence of middle class, middle-aged modes of dress and stultifying forms of morality.

PARIS FASHION

Of course Paris fashion still exists, and in many respects the Paris-based designers are more powerful and make more money than ever before, not because they dictate the new styles, but because they are free to experiment. The clothes that they create aren't dictated by the marketplace because they aren't made to be sold. They are made to create publicity for the lucrative worldwide franchise arrangements into which the majority of couture houses have entered, with the profits rolling in from the perfumes, hosiery, eye-wear, scarves and luggage which carry their name or logo.

Freedom from financial restraint has meant that couture fashion has now entered an era of independence, as voiced by Yves Saint Laurent in the mid-1970s: "In our clothing we have reached complete freedom of expression. There is a spirit of total liberation. Before, women followed our *diktats*. Now there are no *diktats*, and they will never return." St Laurent had stated somewhat earlier in his career: "Haute couture prices make haute couture clothes possible only for the sort of woman no-one wants to look like anymore." And when he introduced his *provocative chic* fashions, which featured cinched waists, spiked heels and the glitter and allure of sexual styling, he claimed these fashions were "for the woman of the future."

▲ *Paris fashion houses often stage spectacular shows displaying extreme fashions — a successful device to attract public attention while indirectly advertising the vast array of perfumes, skincare products and accessories bearing the designer label*

New fashions have to shock the eyes in order to open them.
Pierre Cardin *1981*

▲▲▲ *Fine clothing is a tradition for the Royals. Future kings Edward VIII and George VI would appear in elaborate costume for their afternoon walk in Kensington Gardens, and Elizabeth II ensured that her attire was always impeccable by appointing as her dressmaker Norman Hartnell, the famous London couturier of the 1930s, whose understanding of women's fashion is seen in this dress [right] from his 1934 collection*

Regal Style

In the not-too-distant past, royalty and the aristocracy dictated the dress styles of the day, and they preserved their right to do so by means of elaborate sumptuary laws which restricted various styles of dress, fabrics, colours, accessories and jewellery to specific members of society. But times change and attitudes towards clothing have also changed, thus dramatically affecting the role of royalty and the aristocracy in western society.

THE NON-FASHION FASHION

In most countries the royal families have become totally irrelevant or have disappeared altogether. However, where they remain as figureheads, wardrobe advisers realize that a regal position requires not a display of extravagant consumer wealth but a reassuring continuity, expressed in a style of dress which keeps up with change but distances itself from the particular fripperies of the current mode.

This has allowed the so-called elite to build up a distinct non-fashion style of dress which clearly distinguishes between those who know the exclusive dress rules — i.e. those who are born within the aristocratic non-fashion orientated group — and those of new wealth who tend to display that wealth in new forms of clothing. Money being of lesser importance than lineage, the style of dress is intentionally divisive: it is a style impossible to copy by those born outside the aristocratic group as the rules are constantly, if subtly, changing.

▲ *Before Lady Diana Spencer became engaged to Prince Charles, her non-fashion dress style clearly denoted her aristocratic status*

▲ *The classic Burberry is a favourite with the aspiring rich as its plainness echoes the non-fashion look of the aristocracy*

▼ *Lady Diana Spencer's image rapidly changed when she became a member of the royal family. The non-descript classics were swapped for eye-catching haute couture in order to differentiate the Princess from her previous peer group and accentuate her femininity. The plunge necklines such as this one which bared the traditional display area of Western women — the shoulders and face — were considered by some to be rather risqué*

NUMBER ONE FAMILY

Interestingly enough, in recent years some members of the British royal family have distanced themselves from this elite non-fashion stance for two distinct reasons. Firstly, they do not need a secretly-evolved dress code as their lineage is not in question. They *are* the Number One Family. Secondly, their position as Number One Family rests on their being regarded as separate from their subjects, yet still identifiable with them. Members of the aristocracy on the other hand are now generally regarded as private citizens and may dress as they please according to their own sartorial rules.

In the case of Elizabeth II, this has resulted in her very conservative yet popularly acceptable style of dress. In her younger days before the death of her father and her subsequent coronation she had much more freedom in matters of dress than she has today. As a girl her mother had her instructed in all the distinctly feminine arts, including the use of cosmetics and dress. As a teenager she was allowed to wear an all-in-one bathing costume and high-heeled shoes. She was fitted for an uplift bra, she wore dresses with tight waists. Her jackets often featured large hip pockets which further emphasized her narrow waist. She wore jodhpurs which clearly delineated her

▲ *So accustomed were they to their cumbersome royal attire that George V and Queen Mary displayed no signs of fatigue during their state visit to India in the summer of 1911*

Hats are a sexual lure.
Peter Jago, Milliner, *1987*

▼ *The clothing style of the aristocracy and those royals not in the immediate line of succession is traditional in the extreme and almost impossible to copy. This visibly differentiates between the very highest levels of aristocracy and the aspiring rich who tend to display their wealth in fashion-orientated styles*

legs and indicated that she straddled a horse — a heinous sin in the eyes of the church earlier this century. And her dresses utilized fashionable bust darts and figure shaping.

After her father died, she succeeded him to the throne and appointed Norman Hartnell as her chief dressmaker. Hartnell was a fashionable designer in London during the 1930s and 40s who had dressed many fashion and theatrical personalities — he had even designed scanty feather and sequinned costumes for night-club dancers as well as sumptuous numbers for film stars. In other words, he knew the power and the limits of dress, and he dedicated himself to evolving a dress style for Queen Elizabeth II which would be distinctive and fashionable, yet not identical to or measurable against the current mode.

During these early years of her reign, the Queen wore shorter skirts than any previous monarch had ever dared to do. She wore high-heeled shoes, some with peep toes. She wore hats which drew attention to her face and to every movement of her head. Her dresses often featured a tight waist and a scooped-out neckline. She wore earrings, lipstick and perfume, all of which had been condemned by the Church only a few years earlier as 'sexual' and 'lustful.'

◀ In 1949, before her coronation, the then Princess Elizabeth was often seen wearing typical dress of the period. Styles like the one shown focussed the observer's attention on the fashionable ankle strapped, platform-soled, peep-toe shoes and on to her brimmed hat, thus emphasising feet and face — two of the most important feminine features

DI, FERGIE AND ANNE

The Queen's two daughters-in-law, The Princess of Wales and the Duchess of York have quite different styles of dress. Princess Diana is considered the more fashionable of the two, although she has had to mellow her style in more recent times. It is of interest to recall, however, that it is not so long ago that she favoured tight jeans, see-through dresses and evening styles which looked as if they might just slip off. She was a member of the British aristocracy and, previous to her engagement to Prince Charles had dressed according to their prevailing non-fashion code. On her engagement, however, it was essential that she distance herself from the established mode of aristocratic dress as she was about to become a member of the Number One Family — and possibly even Queen one day. For a time, she dressed in fashionable and even controversial styles which made headlines around the world. After her wedding however, her dress style began to change under the influence of the royal family, and following the birth of her first child public opinion also changed, and this change was soon to be reflected in her mode of dress. She was now perceived as a mother, and mothers must dress in a somewhat more conservative mode.

It is of interest to note that as the Queen's daughter, Princess Anne is no longer in direct succession to the throne, and as her mode of dress is no longer under the scrutiny of the press, her clothes now reflect the prevailing attitudes of the British aristocracy. Her style of dress is anonymous, but easily recognizable by her peers, a style which reflects her love of horses and country life.

Princess Diana on the other hand is still very much at the centre of public interest. As a mother and a future Queen, extremes of fashion have had to be discarded in favour of more socially acceptable modes of dressing. But this does not mean that Princess Diana's mode of dress ceases to convey any sexual messages. The fact is her mode of dress conveys very distinct sexual messages, and it is intended to do so — just as the clothes worn by the Queen also convey sexual messages. Of course these signals are not blatant but they clearly state, via their clothing, that the wearers are female, that they have prestige and power, that they are upholders of tradition, and that they are aware of, and in some cases well above, current fashion trends.

Never fear being vulgar — just boring, middle-class or dull.
Diana Vreeland *1982*

Even when we say nothing, our clothes are talking noisily to everyone who sees us, telling them who we are, where we come from and what we like to do in bed.
The Sunday Telegraph, 1982

SORTING OUT THE MEN FROM THE GIRLS

The easing of many of the censorship laws relating to sexual matters in the 1950s, the growing demand for individual rights following the political upheavals of the 1960s and the rise of feminism and the Women's Rights Movement in the 1970s, have all had a flow-on effect of liberating non-conformist attitudes. One of the results of this has been that cross-dressing and transsexuality have become the centre of comment.

YOURS OR MINE?

Cross-dressing, or *Eonism* as Havelock Ellis calls this particular phenomenon (after Chevalier D'Eon de Beaumont the famous 18th century French spy, who dressed in female clothes whilst on official assignments) is not new. It is an ancient art which has been openly accepted in many societies and condemned in others. In Ancient Greece, for instance, males were allowed and even encouraged to dress as females during the great Athenian festivals, and this was also the case during Roman

▲ *The 18th century French spy D'Eon de Beaumont adopted women's clothing for much of his life in order to operate within the court of the Russian Empress Elizabeth*

▲ Although satirists jibed at the corsets and lace-frilled shirts worn by fashionable gentlemen of the 1820s the desire was never to mimic the female, but add refinement to the male form

▼ 1975 saw a rash of men in ladies' underwear with the release of The Rocky Horror Show in which actor Tim Curry played a seductive transsexual, Frank N Furter, who was partial to black stockings and suspenders

▲ *The Euzones soldier's gathered skirt — like the Scotsman's kilt — denotes strength and masculinity and is worn with great pride*

times. It would appear from numerous references to such modes of dress in the Bible that the Israelites and early Christians did not admire such behaviour. It was obviously somewhat of a problem in those times, as Moses in Deuteronomy felt it necessary to command: "a woman shall not wear that which appertaineth to a man, nor shall a man wear that which appertaineth to a woman. This is an abomination."

WOMEN IN TROUSERS

Today, there is a strange one-sided view of cross-dressing in western society as a whole: most people seem to accept that it is allowable for a women to wear that which appertaineth to a man. They accept quite happily that her reasons are not because she wishes to look like a man but because men's clothing is warmer, or more comfortable, or better suited to travel, or smarter and more businesslike, which of course makes it acceptable for a woman to wear a man's clothes without her being thought a sexual deviant.

▲▲ *In 1851 Amelia Bloomer's attempts to introduce a 'rational mode of dress for women' were condemned by those in positions of authority. Only in relatively recent times have ladies' trousers become widely accepted*

▲ Many respected actors have appeared as women on stage and screen, often stunning the audience with their carriage, and upstaging the leading female beauties of the day!

▼ Cross-dressing does not always deny gender; some transvestites retain their facial hair as an affirmation of masculinity

MEN IN SKIRTS

A man on the other hand, who wishes to wear a dress because it is more comfortable, better to travel in, smarter or more businesslike is thought of as perverse, regarded with deep suspicion and is liable to be beaten up.

This was not the case in 16th century England, however, when it was an established practice for many actors to play the theatrical roles of women, and to live their lives as women in order to create these roles realistically. In fact there were several famous theatrical companies which specialized in training and disciplining young boys in the art of female impersonation for the stage. These boys — generally from well-established theatrical families — were taken into training as actresses at an early age and instructed in the art of make-up, feminine gestures, wearing female apparel, voice control,

▲ The traditional long robes of ecclesiastics are in no way derivative of female dress but are based on the everyday male attire of times gone by

and many were castrated in order to retain their high voices and youthful looks. Their talents were highly respected and they pursued their profession with great zeal, progressing from simple walk-on parts to the more difficult female roles according to their talent and experience. By 1660 the serious art of female impersonation had begun to wane after Margaret Hughes had successfully played the role of Desdemona and, once again, it became an 'abomination' for men to dress as women, even on the stage.

However, once women became established on the stage they were soon dressing as men. There were reports of, for example, an actress's legs being "revealed in a close-fitting male habit, which gave the audience a view of the exact turn of the shape, as complete as if seen without any habit on at all, exhibiting her person in a form more voluptuous and degrading than nakedness itself."

▲ There are many cases of both men and women masquerading as the opposite gender with great success — some for an entire lifetime

◀▲ *Some argue that the growing numbers of utterly convincing transvestites and she-males, many with artificially formed female features, has had a subconscious effect upon today's women, making them more eager to expose the unmistakable soft curves of the genuine article*

▲ *A highly respected tailor of over 35 years experience in London's Savile Row recently revealed that around 25% of his upper class male customers wear some form of female apparel beneath their business suits. This estimate was confirmed by other tailors as well as wholesalers and retailers of lacy lingerie — which is now widely stocked in gents' sizes*

TOP HATS AND SUSPENDERS

Film and television have helped to change attitudes towards clothing styles previously firmly established in people's minds as symbolic forms of nudity and sexual deviation. In the 1930s to 1950s film became the vehicle for a form of feminine exhibitionism sparked off by Marlene Dietrich in *The Blue Angel*. Even today a glimpse of her in top hat, tightly-fitting tail-coat, high-heels, frilly knickers, black stockings and suspenders, huskily singing *Falling In Love Again*, opens up a whole world of eroticism and fetishistic modes of dress for new generations of admirers.

This blatant eroticism and fetishism in clothing is not of the pathological kind of which Krafft and Ebing so skillfully wrote. Rather it is a kind of symbolic eroticism and fetishism in which everybody can partake. In the past many sexual unions between married couples were conducted in the dark beneath the sheets in almost clinical silence. All the nuances of foreplay, often accompanied by exotic and erotic finery, were reserved for professional girls who worked in the more fashionable bordellos. It is from these bordellos that the sexual aura surrounding high-heeled leather boots, black fish-net stockings, suspender belts, laced corsets, leather straps with metal studs and chains, frilly knickers and numerous other items of apparel originated.

Today, we enjoy a more open and honest approach to our changing sexual needs, and many people are experiencing the excitement of wearing some of these items during sexual encounters both within the matrimonial home and outside it. The realization that it is possible to apparently change identity by the simple means of changing one's clothes has come as a revelation.

Many couples find it sexually stimulating to reverse the sexual role from the traditional aggressive male and passive female, sometimes involving the male dressing in female lingerie and the female in traditional male attire. Many people enjoy wearing these erotic styles whether they are male, female or see themselves as somewhere in between the two. Once enjoyed, the clothes themselves become symbols of sexual fulfillment and they spread into daily use where they add variety and visual excitement to current street fashions.

Changing Attitudes

ur current clothing styles may not be perfect, but they are nevertheless the collective expression of our society and they are the best we could do in the circumstances. They also happen to be the standard by which we measure all other clothing styles: those of the rest of the world; of our own past and even of the future. This very act of comparison tends to confuse us, as we find it difficult to perceive ourselves in a mode of dress that strikes us as unsuitable. We tend to think that our current way of dressing is the only way, the natural way, almost an extension of our own bodies, and we find it almost impossible to view other modes of dress objectively. Yet we still have an apparent unwillingness to continue with one style for very long, and our obvious dissatisfaction expresses itself in an appetite for constant change — a kind of chain reaction created by the eternal compromise between modesty and display.

▼ After many years of struggle, western women have won the right to swim and sunbathe topless on most beaches, but society still exercises its taboos on the genital area

▲Unfortunately for the reputation of the French couturiers at the
beginning of the1980s, the majority of their paying customers were
middle-aged and stout, which is one of the reasons why young
street fashions eclipsed Paris's haute couture. Illustration by
Fernando Botero for French Vogue, 1982

▲ The preferred shape of the female form fluctuates. Rubens' Three Graces would be considered a little lumpen today

▲ The display of male nudity is tolerated in our society, but confined to single sex audiences with no minors present

THE SOCIAL NUDE

There are signs that our attitudes are changing. People are displaying their bodies on the beach in the skimpiest of costumes and at keep fit classes in tight, body-revealing leotards. But in general such modes of display are confined to those who are secure in the knowledge that their bodies conform to the current western ideals of beauty. Those bodies which do not conform to the current standard are exercised and starved and invariably kept covered.

CHACUN A SON GOUT

Not all people have the same ideals of beauty. Some women do not like over-developed biceps or muscular thighs on a man but prefer their partners to be more rotund; whilst some men prefer more curves on the female form than is the accepted norm today. A look back at the opulent female figures of Rubens' day compared to the reed-like figures of the 14th century and today, gives some idea of the range of masculine preference in such matters. It must also be accepted of course, that not all men are attracted by members of the opposite sex, whilst not all women seek the company of men, some preferring a close attachment to members of their own sex.

▲ Female breasts are the size and shape they are, not because they have developed that way for feeding babies, but because they are important during sexual display to attract the attention of a number of males so that the most suitable one can be selected as a mate. Here Jayne Mansfield is displaying and Ronald Reagan is paying attention

HAS MODESTY HAD ITS DAY?

Cultural traditions regarding modesty and nudity around the world are changing. People have become disillusioned by middle-class ethics. They are not particularly excited by the unadorned naked body; it is the clothed or partly-clothed body which excites them. They also accept that feminine modesty is extremely important in exciting masculine passion and they fully understand Clement of Alexandria's wise observation that such modesty "only resides in the linen that covers the body, and vanishes once the linen has been removed."

Today it is no longer considered a mortal sin for a woman to be seen without her linen covering of modesty. Many actresses are now willing to perform unadorned. Photographs regularly appear in magazines such as *Club International, Men Only* and *Penthouse* of nubile young women who are willing to display their unique physical characteristics. Many fashion

▲▲ *Many women do not choose their male partners for their looks or their physical attributes, but rather for their ability to pay for and maintain a safe and secure nest. It is therefore fair to say that power and riches are powerful aphrodisiacs*

▶ *The shape of the early 70s, epitomised by the waif-like Twiggy. Her slenderness clearly denoted sexual and financial independence*

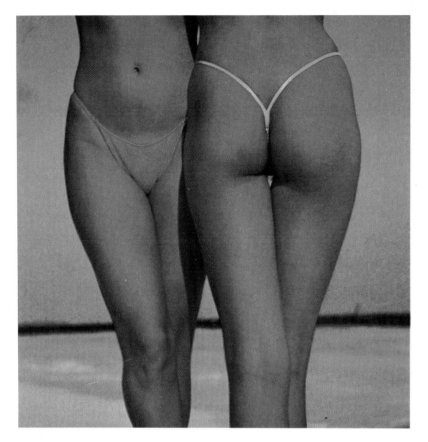

▲ Once the bikini became commonplace, women looked around and found something new in the G-string. What next? Probably it will be the turn of the all-concealing yet figure-revealing one piece

▲ Tits and bums have become commonplace images on billboards and magazine covers, so now it is time to focus attention elsewhere

▶ Admiration for the female form is universal, and whatever fashion may dictate, certain female characteristics never go completely out of style

shows in London, Paris and New York feature bare-breasted and leg-flashing model girls in little more than a chiffon wrap.

SHOWING OFF

Professor Stanley Halls, writing in 1904 stated that: "at puberty there is a natural pride that accompanies the new local developments in the body," and that both young men and women, "glory in occasions when they can display the beauty of their form without reserve." Madame Celine Renooz in 1898 declared: "In the actual life of a young girl today, there is a moment when, by a secret atavism, she feels the pride of her sex, the intention of her moral superiority and cannot understand why she must hide its cause. At this moment, wavering between the laws of nature and social convention, she scarcely knows if nakedness should, or should not affright her. A sort of confused atavistic memory recalls to her a period before clothing was known and reveals to her as a paradisiacal ideal the customs of that human epoch."

FREEDOM OF EXPRESSION FOR WOMEN

The world of sartorial choice is expanding and younger members of society are experimenting with the psychological

In our society the naked body is believed to be incomplete — a body minus clothes. It is the packaged product that we take for the man and the woman.
Bernard Rudofsky *The Unfashionable Human Body, 1972*

power that lies hidden within certain modes of dress. Some young females choose styles which display them as perpetual or even professional virgins. Some wear a more tarty look, whilst others prefer to appear as a male huntress or as a leather-clad dominatrix.

Women have found their horizons broadened by the fashion for wearing tight-fitting exercise leotards. Originally leotards were simply worn for keep fit, but they quickly developed into a legitimate mode for displaying the shapely female as never before. The leotard shapes the waistline, rounds the hips, lifts the bust and emphasizes the pubic area. This not only makes the wearer feel good because of the slight pressure and friction on her clitoris, but makes her look good as well because of her sexual glow — the same sexual glow some girls achieve by wearing tight jeans and our ancestors achieved a hundred years ago by wearing tightly-laced corsets.

PROVOCATION OF LUST

Women are now being more adventurous in choosing fetish items such as tight leather trousers, high-heeled boots, fish-net stockings, decorative garters, suspender belts, and laced-up waist-cinches. These items have become symbols of a fetishism which presents a more imaginative invitation to coital pleasure.

The wearer herself, most psychiatrists agree, is rarely sexually stimulated by the erotic symbolism of these articles of apparel as such. However she invariably enjoys the fiery glances her male partner gives her and she observes with secret gratification the lust he shows for her. And once she has experienced the power of these erotic symbols, she tries to make the maximum use of all of her clothing — not necessarily by wearing provocative fetish modes all the time — but by wearing the more adventurous current fashion trends that have in some way incorporated this form of symbolism.

Women who dress in this new more permissive style are not necessarily prostituting themselves. Western style beauty has always been closely associated with carnal pleasure, and women of fashion throughout the ages have been aware of this basic fact. Even the most concealing styles were never intended to deny the gender of the wearer, but rather to raise the passions of members of the opposite sex. There is a great deal of truth in Robert Burton's contention made in *The Anatomy of Melancholy* more than two centuries ago: "The greatest provocations of lust are from our apparel."

▲ ▶ *Many young women are beginning to experiment with the inherent erotic qualities of leather and rubber, high heels and tight lacing*

▲ *Displays of masculinity such as this are still frowned upon by society*

It is the adorned and the partially concealed body, and not the naked body, which acts as a sexual excitant.

Havelock Ellis *Studies in the Psychology of Sex, 1901*

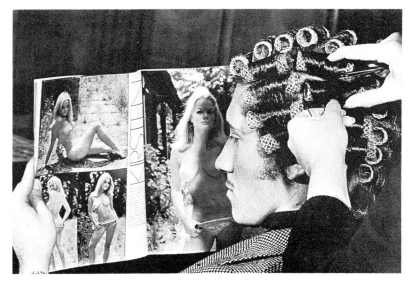

▲ *Men are just as vain about their appearance as women, but in most societies men who curl their hair or wear clothes in attractive colours are considered highly suspect*

FREEDOM OF EXPRESSION FOR MEN

Attitudes regarding the sexuality of men as well as women are changing and these changes are being signalled in their clothing. But whereas women's clothing has become more blatantly sexual as if to signal their sexual liberation, male clothing tends to remain rather conservative except amongst those who prefer the exclusive company of other males, or who are willing to display a certain bisexual ambivalence.

Such males, freed from the previous oppressive laws governing homosexuality, are no longer frightened of being arrested. They openly signal their bisexual or homosexual tendencies, and adopt transvestite and androgynous clothing styles. However, this very fashionability tends to force other males, who do not wish to be identified as either homosexual or bisexual, into an avoidance of any style which might cast doubt upon their sexual prowess and preferences. And whilst many females actually like the new male sartorial modes — particularly those of an androgynous nature — they nevertheless actively discourage their male partners from wearing them.

Male nudity is also suppressed by the weight of public opinion for much the same reason: it has been generally and traditionally accepted that women are not interested in such displays, and that only homosexual and bisexual males find them of interest. Recent research has found this belief to be quite inaccurate, and tests on the automatic dilation of the pupil of the female eye, which is only brought about by keen sexual interest, has shown that most women are just as

▲ *Studded black leather and chains, once the badge of the macho bikie, is a look now favoured by the more adventurous gay males as well as those of androgenous or sado-masochistic inclinations*

sexually interested in a well-proportioned nude male as most males are in a well-proportioned naked female.

In the realms of male clothing and in male sexual display, the weight of public opinion and the law takes much longer to change than it does in response to women's demands. To a large extent, what men wear will depend on the women in their lives. Those males who have no such constraints may soon be able to wear whatever they like, whenever they like — except that, in the foreseeable future at least, their penis, if not their scrotum will have to be hidden from public view.

THE NEED FOR CHANGE

The clothed society has become self-perpetuating. The clothing styles we wear beget more clothes in an unending array, and our current styles are a compromise between the established powers of law-makers, manufacturers and those who control the media and the aspirations and ideas of each new generation who rightfully demand the freedom to dress as they decide.

This is why changes in the western way of dress, particularly those requiring a shift in society's moral attitudes (such as wearing a topless bathing costume or a see-through chiffon blouse without a bra, as in the late 1960s) always take a little longer than the more adventurous would like.

But changes do eventually take place in the way people dress and the physical attributes they are allowed to display or must conceal. Traditions change and change again as each new generation seeks to establish its own sartorial code.

This will continue to be the western way of things until we are once again willing to accept ourselves as complete beings in our natural naked state with no need to conceal our bodies behind our clothing fantasies, *except when we so choose.* Only then will we be willing and tolerant enough to allow the younger members of our society to dress and decorate their bodies as they please, and even to display and highlight their particular nubile charms if they see fit to do so.

A NEW SYMBOLISM

A growing number of young people are developing a style which represents a new attitude towards western style dressing. Aware that, traditionally, nearly all feminine sexual emphasis has been placed on what is perceived as western woman's most attractive features — the face, the shoulders and the breasts — they are attempting to down-grade these traditional areas of erotic symbolism.

▲ As the world grows more conformist, many individualists will choose to dress not necessarily to attract a partner of their choice, but to display their uniqueness

This is a radical departure from the accepted way of things. Traditionally-minded people react strongly against the unusual hairstyles and facial make-up which are not intended to be pretty; the multiple and oddly assorted earrings; the discordant fabrics; the random cutting and mixing of tops over skirts; the apparent jumble of accessories and the exposure of various parts of the female body which traditionally have been kept under wraps.

The older generation sees nothing sexually alluring in the new younger styles because they do not understand the new code. However, these new styles do carry a sexual message: a declaration of youth and nubility. Their body displays announce: "This area is attractive but only amongst ourselves, and is not intended to be attractive to the older members of society." They are also saying: "If you want female lips to be virginal echoes then you are not for us." They do not use eye make-up as a sexual lure but rather to express an attitude to life. They have begun to develop a new form of tribal symbolism the importance of which is that the members of their *tribe* find each other sexually attractive for who they are, not for how pretty they look.

▲ *Professional ready-to-wear designers are responsible for producing billions of dollars-worth of new fashion each year. To be successful they must make styles that people are willing to pay for. That doesn't mean that they should produce only cheap styles, because people are prepared to pay the extra $50 for a pair of Calvin Klein jeans provided they fit better, or are better styled and project the image the wearer has of him or herself more successfully than those of a rival brand*

Fashion is a form of free speech and one of the privileges, if not always one of the pleasures of living in a free world.
The Sunday Telegraph, 1982

THE FASHION INDUSTRY

Fashion, some critics say, is simply a method used by certain members of society to flaunt their wealth at the expense of the rest of the world: a device aimed at preventing other more important social changes from taking place.

To some extent these critics could well be right in that a preoccupation with materialism deflects energy away from more important social issues.

COMMERCIAL CONSPIRACY

Other critics believe that changeable fashions are simply a cunning confidence trick: that all new fashionable styles are unilaterally agreed upon by the unscrupulous manufacturers before being imposed on a waiting and gullible public.

Indeed, in America alone, nearly $25 billion worth of men's and women's fashions were wholesaled in 1985. But only a

---

Today the clothes that we choose to wear can reveal many aspects about us — what our age is, where we are going, where we live, and, often, what we do for a living.
Lucille Khornak *Fashion 2001, 1982*

MIX AND MATCH

▲ The disdainful style of London's Sloane Rangers is unattractive to some, but sexually provocative to their peer group

▲ Well-styled mix and match separates were an inspired fashion idea that found a ready market throughout the world

▼ Famous people cannot afford to ignore the image game. Margaret Thatcher projects a feeling of being in complete control of her hair, her make-up and her cabinet colleagues

▼ Many European peoples find their own traditional styles attractive, particularly in countries such as Germany, Austria and Switzerland

Bogner

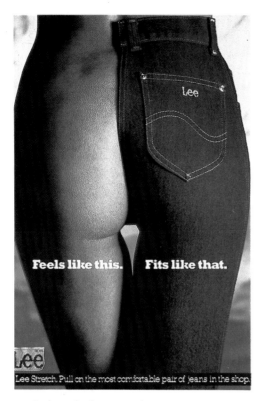

Feels like this. | Fits like that.

Lee Stretch. Pull on the most comfortable pair of jeans in the shop.

▲ *Styles which restrict the wearer in some way have always been successful*

part of this vast fortune awaits those whose merchandise fulfills the desires of the customers; others are forced into bankruptcy. Manufacturers are in fact in deadly competition with each other.

DESIGN FOR WEARING

To be successful, most manufacturers employ a team of designers, each specializing in a different facet of the fashion range produced. Designers must know the practical possibilities of their ideas and how these ideas fit into the new season's scheme. Their designs must show a clear contemporary feeling and reflect, in some way or other, the subconscious undercurrents of everyday life. This feeling — this talent of extra-sensory perception — is a basic essential for every fashion designer. It cannot be taught, it can only be encouraged, made more practical and more commercial.

Unfortunately, practical and commercial are often thought of as dirty words. But it must be realized that a fashion designer is part of a commercial enterprise. The job is to produce designs which the paying public wish to purchase today — they do

▲▲ *Borrowed styles: shoulder pads do not make a woman look masculine, on the contrary they emphasise the slenderness of her neck and the delicacy of her bone structure and add to her feminine appeal. Plundering the styles of the past also provides a good excuse to look sexy*

not want to wait until next year, or even to next month to buy the latest design styles, because next year these fashions will be old and dusty curiosities.

TIME FOR CHANGE

Manufacturers and designers must never rest on their past successes, as they are only as good as this season's range, and they must always be willing to change. One year the accent of fashion may be 'dressing for success' and the following year 'street fashions' or 'affluent styles' may take over.

Many designers specialize in just one area of design, pinpointing the kind of customer who will respond to their particular look: the 18 to 22 year-old who buys new clothes because they are fun; the career woman of 25 to 35 years of age who is co-habiting and has a thriving social life; the married woman with several children; the sportswoman or the fashion trendsetter who loves to wear the very latest in fashionable styles. A designer's job is then to sense whether the women or men in their area of specialization want more of the same or are ready for a radical change.

▲ It is difficult now to imagine a time when flamboyant fashions were the sole prerogative of the royal courts. For many young people today fashion provides a creative outlet that helps them cope with the pressures of life

Ridicule and scorn are the sanctions which force people to follow fashion, and the dissenter is powerless before them.
Elizabeth B Hurlock 1929

◀ Buy! buy! buy! scream the adverts, and buy, buy, buy is what we do. The exhilaration of spending money coupled with the envy we feel when faced with an item we think we need, are the main motives for buying fashion products

▲ *Off-the-peg fantasies for sale in the form of erotic underwear — no one will buy one of these just because they need a new pair of knickers*

> *Too much practical lingerie makes a dull woman. An occasional frill or trimming of lace is good for the soul.*
>
> *Vogue, 1932*

> *Body fashions are, above all, a matter of aesthetics. A woman today who chooses to re-make her body by exercise may be developing a more efficient living machine, but she is also redefining the boundaries of femininity. One man's Helen of Troy is another mans sideshow hermaphrodite.*
>
> Newspaper comment on women body builders *1983*

Designers who can instinctively find their way through this maze are admirably suited to continue the tradition of designing exciting, unusual, and controversial fashion styles well into the 21st century.

STREET FASHION

In recent years there has been a great influx into the fashion industry of talented but untrained 'street designers' who have helped rejuvenate the world of fashion by their innovative approach to young dressing. Young journalists have joined the established magazines to help promote these new younger styles. New breeds of fashion photographer and fashion illustrator are emerging, and fashion models are becoming more independent and more individual. Gone are the pre-packaged *Barbie* dolls of yesteryear.

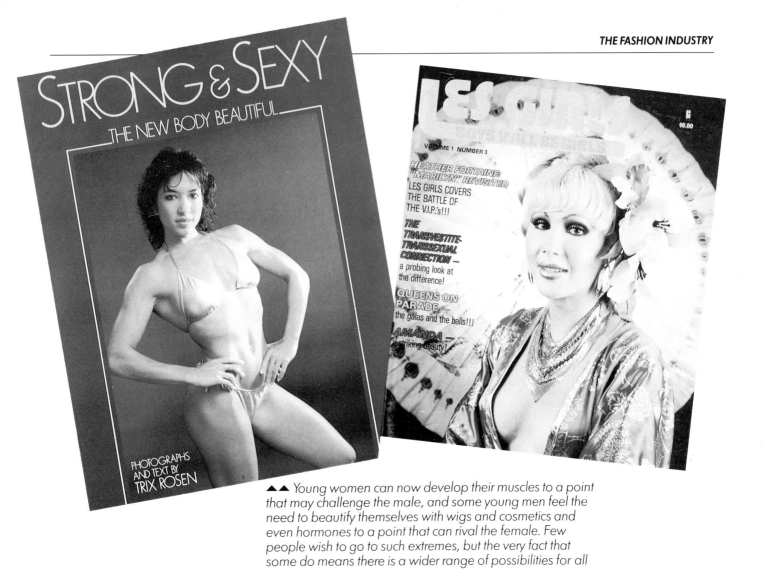

▲▲ *Young women can now develop their muscles to a point that may challenge the male, and some young men feel the need to beautify themselves with wigs and cosmetics and even hormones to a point that can rival the female. Few people wish to go to such extremes, but the very fact that some do means there is a wider range of possibilities for all*

Thus it appears that fashion will continue to become more innovative, younger, sexier and much more independent. The fashions of the 21st century may well be even more sexually provocative than those being currently worn.

THE SHAPE OF THINGS TO COME

Yves Saint Laurent predicts that women will be willing to wear more sexy fashions, and the American Bill Blass believes that the whole structure of American dress will soon change as women will have more courage and individuality. "But," he says, "the big change will be at night towards more dramatic, sexy and bizarre styles." He also believes that in America clothes will accentuate the difference between "the affluent and the non-affluent, the haves and have-nots."

Fetish styles will become widely accepted (established couples will continue to interest their chosen mate by changing clothes, rather than changing partners); new trends will also develop out of the ever-increasing range of music videos; transvestite dressing and she-male fashions will continue, with males dressing as women but never denying their masculinity,

No women ever really dresses *for a man — men like their women undressed. For men, the naked female animal has fur and smell and secretion and flush enough.*
Gina Lurie 1976

POP ART

MARY QUANT

▲ Women learn very early in life that dressing up in a certain way and projecting a particular image can help them to be what they want and to get what they want

▼ Because of the associations we have about tattoos and women, we find it difficult to see a tattoo as an attractive adornment

just as some women dress as men yet never deny their femininity. And, no doubt, some clothes will be expressly designed to indicate the degree of heterosexual or homosexual orientation of the wearer.

INDIVIDUALITY

Fashion is likely to become much more individual. This will create problems for the manufacturers and the stockists who from time to time have appeared unwilling or unable to adapt their styles to changing times. This will create opportunities for new or little-known manufacturers to produce new ranges of clothes and a wider range of fashionable choice.

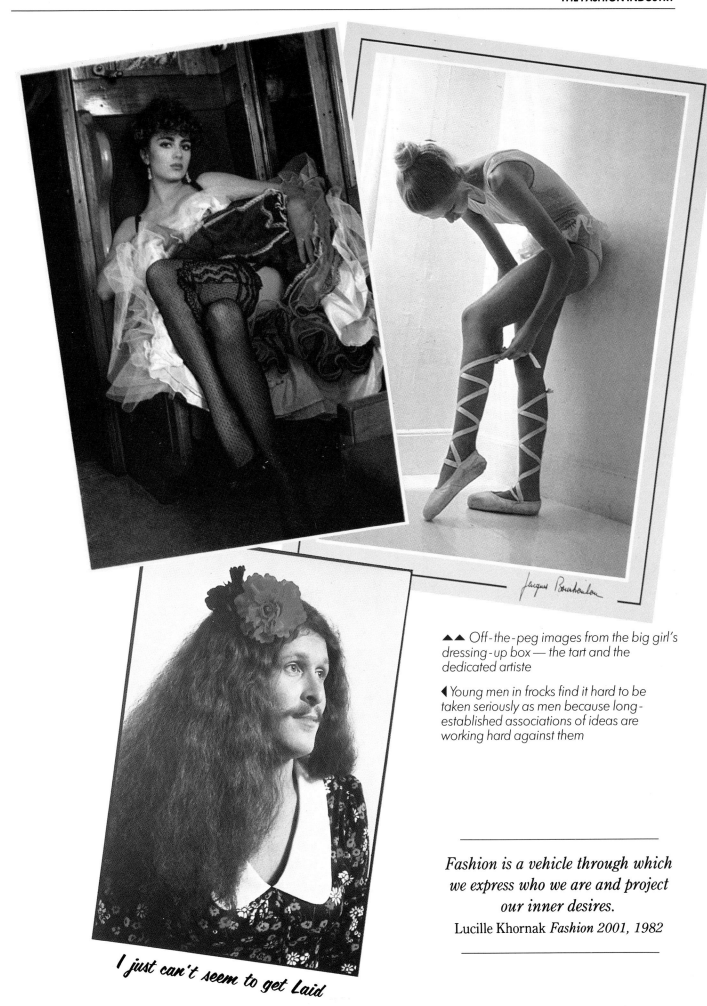

Jacques Bourboulon

▲▲ Off-the-peg images from the big girl's dressing-up box — the tart and the dedicated artiste

◀ Young men in frocks find it hard to be taken seriously as men because long-established associations of ideas are working hard against them

I just can't seem to get laid

Fashion is a vehicle through which we express who we are and project our inner desires.
Lucille Khornak *Fashion 2001, 1982*

HOPES AND DREAMS

But major changes in our ways of dress do not come about because designers' ideas change, or because manufacturers start producing new ranges of merchandise, or even because the laws on dress change. They are just symptoms of a changing society, the result of varying influences — economic climate, education, work patterns, entertainment, the mass-media, wars — all of which change people's hopes, aspirations, ideals, moral attitudes and their day-dreams about the future way of things.

In this context our day-dreams are most important. Just as ethnic people hope to alter their lives by adopting western modes of dress, people in the west 'dream' of transforming themselves by wearing clothes that symbolize their ideals. This symbolic change is the most visually conspicuous of the mechanisms by which we hope to alter ourselves and our way of life. Social commentators have noted with great interest how our bodies actually seem to change over the years in response to changing fashions and changing times.

INTERPRETING THE MOOD

Designing fashion takes talent, intelligence and instinct as well as sound knowledge of construction methods, marketing and finance. It takes a special ability to create the kind of clothes women of different body types like, will buy and can happily wear if such styles are going to be mass produced. A designer also requires the ability to create publicity and hype.

Paul Poiret remarked in *En Habillant l'Epoque* (1930): "When a woman chooses a dress, she believes her choice is free and personal, which of course it isn't. It's the mood of fashion that inspires and guides her impulses." The designer must interpret that mood correctly, as even the most devoted customers will not buy the new styles if they do not like them.

But such a choice is by no means completely individual or free. Our western culture tends to be very conformist and imposes certain codes on our modes of dress that reflect the prevailing mood, morals, mores, beliefs and attitudes of our age. If a manufacturer is able to capture all of this, and then add a touch of individual wit or panache, then he will produce designs to meet all of our changing needs.

WHAT NEXT?

For many young people clothing styles have become a form of performance art, capable of voicing dissent and deviance from the previously socially accepted norm.

The idea of feminine beauty is not an unmixed idea; it is intimately united with the idea of carnal pleasure.
Remy de Gourmont *1901*

▶▶ *The games people play for love often include dressing the part, because it is possible to take on a new identity, simply by changing clothes, and leave the old conventional self outside the bedroom door*

▲ *All new ideas in fashion imagery have to be studied by designers and fashion writers who want to stay ahead of the pack. The androgynous look of the late 70s was one that nearly missed the boat because some people had difficulty coming to terms with it, and now it's the turn of a newly-emerging sex, the she-male, whose choice of clothing styles is worthy of study*

▶ *The corset keeps coming back!*

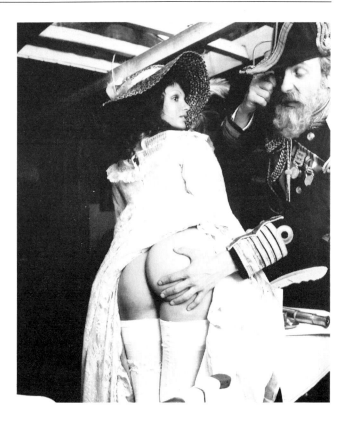

Paris flash:

THE OFF~THE~PEG MOULDED BODY TOP

Issey Miyake went to all lengths, here silken jersey slashed skirts softest gleaming tops of scarlet, bronze (top) and magenta with its swirl of quilted skirts (far left). Kansai's exotic bird that flew west for the collections: imperial purple, scarlet and gold for breastplate, quilted pants and kimono-cut coat (far left). Thierry Mugler's breastplates with chiffon in metallic silver, flame and moss (above and left).

The plastic torso with high-risi breastplate does present a few probler how, for instance, do you bend down the thing, or dance warmly with a m and, given certain circumstances, wh happens when the heat is on? Wil melt? Run? Spread? No matter. It is newest spectacular from Paris and, such, its birth is worth recording. course it has advantages: it is great the flat-chested. It will pack like a dre a dozen stacked flat in a bag will we next to nothing. And so will its supp ing skirt: mini, maxi or whatev Doesn't need ironing. Moths can't ge it. Forget drycleaning. If it takes o and stranger things have happene women may never wear a fabric dr again. Shocked? Take note of the bu It began life as a bum roll in the 1 century, progressed to cork rump in 18th. The Victorians called it dress prover. The French gave it class. T nure they christened it, and the bu was born. Hail plastic torso with hi rising breastplate . . .

▲ *Ever since the early days of rock and roll, teenage fans have been dressing in imitation of their idols. It is the same desire that prompted older generations to imitate Ginger Rogers or Gene Kelly*

▶ *Whilst rock and pop singers have left their mark on young clothing styles, the stars of the multi-million dollar soap-operas have been influencing the older woman with their ritzy, glitzy style and their sexually aggressive image*

Taught from infancy that beauty is women's sceptre, the mind shapes itself to the body and roams round its gilt cage, only seeking to adorn its prison.
Mary Wollstonecraft *1792*

INNER MIRRORS

Elizabeth Wilson points out in her book *Adorned in Dreams* (1985), that what so many young people engage in today "is no longer only the relatively simple process of direct imitation, but the less conscious one of identification." Clothing as a personal art form is also increasing. American artist Tina Girouard, one of the pioneers of *art-to-wear* states: "the erogenous zones of the body are our second *mind*, we think with our bodies as well as with our brains." In a copy of the Italian magazine *Domus* published in the early 1980s she is quoted: "Clothing not only deletes the surface of a person, but somehow also projects his or her soul outside it, revealing the innermost secrets of their personality. Clothes, especially if chosen outside the social conditionings that impose subjection to a given role — when the clothes represent a distinct uniform — can reveal better than any psycho-analytical session the Mr Hyde harboring within each of us . . . furthermore, they act as inner mirrors — as monitors of the hidden ego."

DREAMTIME

In fact many of today's styles are the result of our inner fantasies. They should not be judged on how they look to others, but on how the wearers believe they look in their own minds. These garments are projecting an inner image, however hallucinatory, of how the wearers view themselves. In many instances they adorn the wearers' dreams. This has led to an increase in demand for special occasion, or *performance* clothes to be worn at annual carnivals and mardi-gras, weekend parties, for dancing, playing tennis, exercise classes, sun-baking and swimming, or for weddings or similar social occasions, when we can all dress up and play a specific part in the proceedings, as if we were actors and actresses.

OPERA AND THEATRE

Designers like Karl Lagerfeld and Yves Saint Laurent have helped to emphasize this fantasy element by undertaking design commissions for theatrical productions and then letting this

Clothes are aphrodisiacs for man's vanishing potency.
Dr Edmund Bergler *1953*

▼▼ *In the small print of specialist magazines we read of the excitement that the wearing of black leather affords. Liberated couples are offered the stimulating thrills of bondage styles at a price they can barely afford. It is a close association with bondage gear that has endowed all fashion garments made of black leather with an indefinable erotic quality that adds a great deal to their ultimate allure*

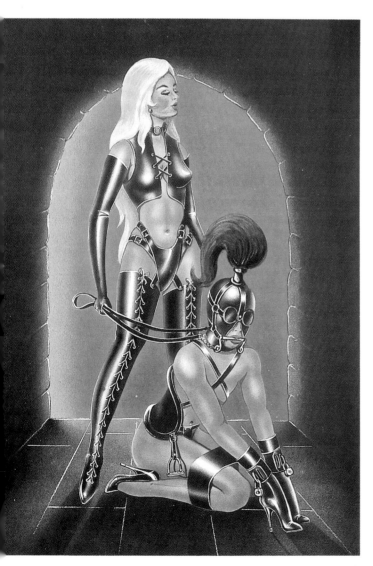

theatrical creativity seep back into their fashion work. Saint Laurent in particular now regards his *haute couture* collections as pure theatre. "Fashion is opera and theatre. It is dreams and phantoms and magic," he says, and his recent collections have been exotic, erotic, sexually alluring and provocative. And

The art of body painting has recently been revived and introduces a contemporary sophistication to this ancient art form

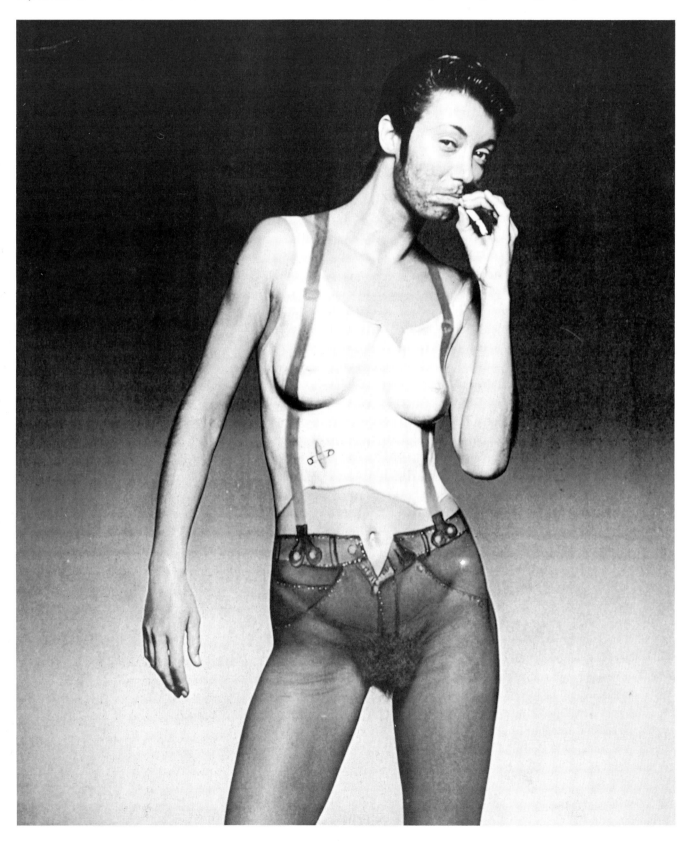

this message has been transmitted around the world by the fashion press and the mass-media. Axel Madsen, Saint Laurent's official biographer described the seasonal Paris fashion shows as "the foremost form of modern live entertainment. Ten days of madness . . . with the big names

▼ Country style clothing is perceived as very sexy because people associate country folk (wrongly as it happens) with very active and varied sex lives

each wanting to stop the parade . . . the city of lights becomes Hollywood-sur-seine — an extravaganza of colour, hysteria and tension, special effects and over-stimulation . . ."

The theatricality and adornment of our dreams is accentuated by television commercials, music video tapes, performance clothes worn by rock and pop artists, and by films aimed at the teenage market — all of which have given rise to distinctive modes of dress intended to clothe the psyche, rather than the body.

A RETURN TO NAKEDNESS?

Unlike Professor J C Flugel, and a number of other eminent sartorial experts, I do not believe that our ultimate destiny is nakedness. I believe that, in the western world at least, there is a natural predisposition to adorn our bodies with a wide range of clothing items and accessories. Regardless of how attractive we might find the nakedness of members of the opposite sex, we as a society could not bear to face the prospect of having to continually look at the naked bodies of others. The present system, I believe, was not originally introduced to totally cover and conceal the body — but was intended to add continual titillation by the process of partial

▲ X-rated movies and videos have added a new dimension to the way people think about their bodies

▶▼ Traditional forms of carnival clothing and make up have influenced the way people dress for parties and other special occasions

exposure and partial concealment, the display and highlighting of our varying physical characteristics.

If we continue to be a clothed society, we must be prepared to defend the right to dress as individuals, exposing or concealing those areas of our bodies which we choose.

Young designers from all over the western world are beginning to reshape our way of thinking about our bodies and our clothes. They have grown up in an industrialized world surrounded by many forms of sexual stimulation and they are aware that our sexual senses have become jaded. They are aware nonetheless that sexual attraction is a very important part of our lives — especially through clothing styles — just as it has always been, ever since the dawn of history. They are aware that there is much more to be understood in the symbolism and sexual associations of a gathered frill and a tantalising section of lace edging, than how it is made, or where it is placed.

IN CELEBRATION OF THE HUMAN FORM

It is my belief that as we approach the end of the 20th century, we will witness the emergence of a new form of experimentation in our styles of body adornments and modes of self-presentation. People in the west will once again come to realize that it is the natural right of the human species to decide on their own mode of dress, particularly during their hours of relaxation. These new styles will be a celebration of our uniquely human bodies — that will best be admired as we strut around on our shapely hind legs, displaying our varying stages of physical development and our varying degrees of sexual excitement. Our faces will no longer be our sole means of communicating our sexual desires and individual aspirations.

Many of these new styles will be works of aesthetic sensibility — to be worn for their own sake by those who wish to be admired for what they are wearing rather than how sexually desirable such garments make them. Whilst those who wish to display their sexual charms will be free to do so in a whole new range of sexually-orientated apparel which will include genital jewellery, and a variety of body aids to enhance the erotic appeal of the wearer's breasts, shoulders, buttocks, thighs, calf muscles, waistline, penis and scrotum or any other parts of the male and female anatomy — just as their ancestors have done since the dawn of time.

And in these new modes our eyes are still going to be far more important than our minds in determining what looks

▲ Not all contemporary modes of dress transmit direct sexual messages, sometimes the messages that come across are of wealth and social status. But they also have sexual connotations because there is a belief amongst those who are not well off that the rich and famous are continually indulging in sex — always at it so to speak

▶ Whatever new forms of body packaging people opt for in the future, you can be sure that they will be accompanied by howls of protest from professional moralists of the time

Today's fashions have no past, no future, they are now. They represent a style of life and express how we live.
Emanuel Ungaro *1981*

appealing, interesting or erotic. Freed from the necessity of having to conform to any arbitrarily imposed rules, we will be able to decide on the *look* alone whether this or that style suits us best.

We have inherited tens of millions of years of ability to distinguish — with our eyes — between the slight differences and nuances of one visual message and another. And I believe that it will be this important ability which will foster our future delights in an enthralling, fascinating, and entirely human preoccupation. And that our dress styles and modes of adornment will continue to embody a uniquely human, coded system that will openly transmit to our fellow beings our individual desires and aspirations.

▶ *As we have seen throughout this book, what was once seen as too shocking to contemplate, is later viewed as perfectly acceptable and later still as outmoded and quaint. This may soon be the case with a garment such as this*

Index

Historical Index

Acknowledgements

Key: [t] top [b] bottom [c] centre [l] left [r] right Julian Robinson JR

4 JR 6 Time/Life, New York 13 Snark International, Paris 14 Walker Art Gallery, Liverpool 15[t] Carol Beckwith 15[b] Ardea, London 16[r] George Melly 17[1] Leni Riefenstahl 17[r] Aubrey Elliott 18 Rapho, Paris / Paolo Curto 20[t] BBC Hulton Picture Library, London 21[c] JR 22[t] Cairo Museum 22[b] St Germaine-en-Laye / Giraudon, Paris 23[t] Zdenek Burian / Artia, Prague 24[b] Bernard Hermann 25[t] Carol Beckwith 25[b] Aubrey Elliott 26[tl] Photo Source, London / Peter Barry 26[tr] Rex Features, London 26[b] V Englebert / ZEFA (Germany) 27[t] T Zimberhoff 27[b] Edizioni Storti, Venice 28[t] Chanel Boutique, London 28[b] Athens Museum 29[t] Matioli, Italy 29[b] National Gallery, London 30[l] Kalvin Klein 30[r] Museum of Modern Art, New York 31[t] Bluebell Organisation / Daniel Frasnay 31[c] Scelo Enterprises 31[b] Brian Aris 32[t] Mary Evans Picture Library, London 33[t] Daily Telegraph Colour Library, London 33[b] Cooper-Bridgeman / Victor Lownes, London 34[t] Photo Source, London 34[bl] JR 34[br] Tatler / David Wright 35[tl] John Kelly 35[tr] Susan Griggs Agency, London 35[c] Nicholas Guppy 35[b] Stephan Richer 36[tl] Scala, Florence 36[tr] National Portrait Gallery, London 36[bc] Lemi Riefenstahl 36[br] Douglas Dickins 37 Dr H Wouters 38 Nat Dallinger 39[b] Louvre, Paris 40 National Gallery, London 41[t] Mansell Collection, London 41[b] Louvre, Paris 42[t] Simone Pèrèle, Paris 42[b] Victoria and Albert Museum, London 43 Magnum, New York 44 Topham Picture Library, London 45[t] Sandra Kauffman 45[b] Real London 47 Victoria and Albert Museum, London 49 JR 50[t] JR 50[b] Louvre, Paris 51[t] JR 52[t] Staatlische Kunstsammlunge, Dresden 53[tl] National Gallery, London 53[bl] JR 53[r] Victoria and Albert Museum, London 54[l] Mary Evans Picture Library, London 54[r] JR 55[b] Musée Carnavalet / Snark International, Paris 57[l] Giraudon, Paris 57[r] Sir Owen Morshead Collection 58[t] JR 58[b] Top Man, London 59[t] Magnum (London) / Bob Adelman 60 Wallace Collection, London 61[l] Mansell Collection, London 61[r] Musée Carnavalet 62 JR 63[b] Club International 64 Club International 65[a] JR 66[ALL] JR 67[b] Phototeque 68[t] Camerapix Hutchinson Library, London 68[c] Sedifo, Geneva 69[tl] Museum of Herakleion, Crete 69[bl] Musée de Cluny, Paris 69[r] JR 70[l] JR 71[tl] New York Public Library 71[tr] New York Public Library 71[b] British Museum, London 72[c] BBC Hulton Picture Library, London 72[b] Fredericks of Hollywood 73 All-Sport, London 74[t] Harper's Bazaar, London 74[b] JR 75[tr;b] JR 76[tl;tr] JR 77[t] JR 77[b] Musée Carnavalet 78 - 82 JR 83 The Kobal Collection, London 84[t] Busby Berkeley / Jim Terry 84[br] The Kobal Collection, London 85[r] Harper's Bazaar, London 86[t] Vogue, Paris 86[tr] Berketex, London 86[b] Horst P Horst 87[t;b] Time/Life, New York 89[tl] Paris Match 89[bl] Harper's Bazaar, London 89[r] House of Dior, Paris 90[tl] Warner Bros. 90[tc] Press Association, London 90[b] Time/Life, New York / M Hansen 91[l] United Press International, New York 93 Harper's Bazaar, London 94 Frank Spooner Pictures, London 95 Maureen Bisilliat 96[br] BBC Hulton Picture Library, London 97[l] Leni Riefenstahl 97[r] Kenneth Anger 98[tl] Malcolm Kirk 98[bl] Aubrey Elliott 98[br] Jean-Louis Nou 99[b] Maureen Bisilliat 100[b] Carol Beckwith 101[b] Fotogram / Lolliot 102[r] C & J Lenars 104[c] The Kobal Collection 104[b] Magnum Archives, Paris 105[b] Epic 106[tl] Black Star (New York) 106[br] Ullstem-Herrnleben 107 Angela Fisher 108 Kunsthistorishes Museum, Vienna 108[b] Aubrey Elliott 109[t] Kenneth Anger 109[c] BBC Hulton Picture Library, London 109[c] Rex Features, London 110[t] C & J Lenars 110[b] C & J Lenars 111[tl] JR 111[tr] Leni Riefenstahl 111[bl] JR 111[br] C & J Lenars 112[b] E Ikonomou 113[t] Mansell Collection, London 113[b] JR 114[tl] Playboy 114[tr] Stefan Richer 114[bl] JR 115 Leni Riefenstahl 116[b] JR 117[t] Teenform Inc. 117[b] Time/Life, New York / J Dominis 118[t] Jenny Wainwright 118[bl] Vogue, Australia 118[br] Mary Evans Picture Library, London 119[t] Jopix, London 119[c] Centurian Publications, California 119[br] The Kobal Collection, London 120[t] Harper's Bazaar, London 120[b] Harper's Bazaar, London 121[c] Centurian Publications, California 122[tl] Angela Fisher 122[b] The Wallace Collection, London 122[b] Brown Bros., New York 123[c] National Gallery of Scotland, Edinburgh 124[bl] Carol Beckwith 124[br] JR 125[t] The Seeberger Brothers, Paris 125[b] Busby Berkley / Jim Terry 126[t] Peter Knapp / Times Newspapers Ltd., London 126[b] Centurian Publications, California 127 Tom Kelly Studio 128[t] BBC Hulton Picture Library, London 128[b] British Museum, London 129[t] Centurian Publications, California 129[b] Harper's Bazaar, London 130[t] BBC Hulton Picture Library, London 130[c] New York Public Library 130[b] Public Records Office, London 131 Bettman Archive, New York 133 Viz, Australia 134[b] Hepworth's, London 135 The Kobal Collection, London 136[bc] Vogue, London / Norman Parkinson 136[br] Harper's Bazaar, London 137[b] BBC Hulton Picture Library, London 138[tl;tr] Daily Telegraph Colour Library, London 138[b] William Claxton 139[l] Myake Design Studio, Tokyo 139[r] Daily Telegraph Colour Library, London 140[t] Camera Press, London 140[b] Vogue, London 141[bl] Syndication International, London 142[t] Camera Press, London 142[b] Photo Source, London 143[b] Time/Life, New York / Bill Ray 144[t] Camera Press, London 145[t] Time/Life, New York 147[rc] EMI Records, London 147[br] Norman Parkinson 148[t] Mayfair / Fisk Pub. Co. Ltd., London 148[c] Paul Raymond 148[b] SPADEM, Paris 149[b] Associated Press 150[tr] Pro Art Inc./ Dallas Football Club 151[t] Bologna & Figli 151[b] High Tide 152[t] Harper's Bazaar, London 152[b] Richard Lawton / Hugo Lecky 153[t] Vogue, London / David Bailey 153[b] Catholic Times [UK] 154[tl] Clive, London 154[tr] Harper's Bazaar, London / Richard Avedon 154[b] Photo Source, London 155[l] Vogue, London 155[r] Photo Source, London 156 Paco Rabann, Paris 157[tl;tc] BBC Hulton Picture Library, London 157[tr] Harper's Bazaar, London 157[b] Press Association, London 158[t] Burberrys of London 158[b] Tim Graham Picture Library, London 159[t] BBC Hulton Picture Library, London 159[b] Serge Lemoine 160 BBC Hulton Picture Library, London 161 Mansell Collection, London 162[t] Guildhall, London 163[b] Harper's Bazaar, London 164[t] Paramount Pictures 164[b] Mansell Collection, London 165[b] Harpers & Queen, London 166 John Kelly 167[b] Centurian Publications, California 169 Statics 170 Photo Source, London 171 Vogue, Paris 172[tl] Prado, Madrid 172[tr] Syndication International, 173[t] The Seeberger Bros., Paris 173[bl] Kenneth Anger

173[r] Richard Avedon 174[l] Photo Source 174[r] Club International 175 Men Only 176 Centurian Publications, California 177[tl] Nelson Photographics, Sydney / Rob Webb 177[tr] Sedifo, Geneva 177[b] Centurian Publications, California 180 Barbara Walz 181[tl] Bob Krieger 181[tr] Harpers & Queen, London 181[bl] Bogner 181[br] Rex Features, London 182[t] Lee 182[bl] Follow Me, Australia 182[br] Popperfoto, London / Pictorial Parade 183[t] Fincom Holdings Ltd., London 183[b] Lotto 184 Fredericks of Hollywood 185[l] Trix Rosen 185[r] Les Girls 186[t] Mary Quant, London 186[b] C Roblewski 187[tl] Men Only 187[tr] Image In Editions / Jacques Bourboulon 187[b] Innovisions, Chicago 188 American Art Enterprises, Hollywood 189[tl] Photo Source, London / Peter Barry 189[tr] Club International 189[b] Mode 190[t] Maybelline 190[b] Lucille Khornak 191[l] Centurian Publications, California 192 Photo Source, London 194[t] Hofbo 194[b] Alexander Orloff 195 Alexander Orloff 196 Sedifo, Geneva 197 Club International 199 Lucille Khornak

We have made every effort to locate and credit the original sources of the illustrations used in this book, many of which were originally selected for use in my Royal College of Art thesis and subsequent college lectures. Through a variety of clues we have been able to attribute most of them, but there are a number we have been unable to trace. I apologise to those persons and organisations whose proprietary or creative interests we have failed to determine and credit. Information brought to the attention of The Watermark Press, 72-80 Cooper Street, Surry Hills, NSW 2010 will be included in all future editions.

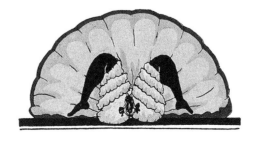

Bibliography

This is by no means a full bibliography; it is merely a selection of books that I have referred to during the course of my research and which I think will be of interest to the reader.

Ackroyd, Peter *Dressing Up: Transvestism and Drag*, London 1979

Adams, Mrs A *Hints on Dress for Ladies*, London 1857

Anderson Black, J & Madge Garland *A History of Fashion*, London 1975

Anonymous *The Habits of Good Society: A Handbook of Etiquette for Ladies and Gentlemen*, London 1865

Anger, Kenneth *Hollywood Babylon*, New York 1975

Barthers, Roland (translated by Matthew Ward & Richard Howard) *The Fashion System*, London 1985

Battersberry, Michael & Ariane *Mirror Mirror: A Social History of Fashion*, New York 1977

Battersby, Martin *The Decorative Twenties*, London 1969

Beaton, Cecil *The Glass of Fashion*, London 1954

Beckwith, Carol & Tepilit Ole Saitoti *Maasai*, London 1980

Beckwith, Carol & Marion Van Offelen *Nomads of Niger*, London 1984

Bell, Quentin *On Human Finery*, London 1976

Berger, John *Ways of Seeing*, London 1972

Bergler, Edmund *Fashion and the Unconscious*, New York 1953

Binder, Pearl *The Peacock's Tail*, London 1958

Birch Ian (editor) *The Book With No Name*, London 1981

Bisillant, Maureen & O C Villas-Bôas *Xingu Tribal Territory*, London 1979

Brain, Robert *The Decorated Body*, London & New York 1973

Brogden, Joanne *Fashion Design*, London & New York 1971

Dickens A G (editor) *The Courts of Europe 1400-1800*, London 1977

Dixon, Terence & Martin Lucas *The Human Race*, London 1982

Edin, Victoria *The Body Decorated*, London 1979

Eichler, Lillian *Customs of Mankind*, New York 1925

Elliott, Aubry *Sons of Zulu*, London & Johannesburg 1978

Ellis, Havelock *Studies in the Psychology of Sex*, Philadelphia 1901/10

Ewing, Elizabeth *History of Human Costume*, London 1977

Fisher, Angela *Africa Adorned*, London 1984

Fisher, Helen E *The Sex Contract: The Evolution of Human Behaviour*, London 1983

Flugel, J C *The Psychology of Clothes*, London 1929

Fraser, Antonia (translator) *Dior by Dior: The Autobiography of Christian Dior*, London 1957

Fryer, Peter *Mrs Grundy: Studies in English Prudery*, London 1963

Garland, Madge *The Changing Form of Fashion*, London 1970

Garland, Madge *The Changing Face of Beauty*, London 1975

Glynn, Prudence *Skin to Skin: Eroticism in Dress*, London 1980

Glynn, Prudence *In Fashion: Dress in the Twentieth Century*, London 1978

Greer, Germaine *The Female Eunuch*, London 1971

Griagoriev S L (translated by Vera Bowen) *The Diaghilev Ballet 1909-1929*, London

Hartman, Rose *Birds of Paradise: An Intimate View of the New York Fashion World*, New York, 1980

Hartnell, Norman *Silver and Gold*, London 1955

Haviland, William A *Anthropology*, New York 1974

Hennessy, Val *In the Gutter*, London 1978

Bronowski, J *The Ascent of Man*, London 1973

Burian, Zdenek & Josef Wolf *The Dawn of Man*, London 1978

Carlyle, Thomas *Sartor Resartus*, London 1833

Carter, Ernestine *Twentieth Century Fashion*, London 1975

Carter, Ernestine *The Changing World of Fashion*, London 1977

Challamel, M Augustin *A History of Fashion in France*, Paris & London 1882

Chesterfield, Lord, & others (compiled from) *Encyclopaedia of Manners and Etiquette for Young Men*, London 1884

Clark, Sir Kenneth *The Nude: A Study in Ideal Form*, London 1956

Clark, Sir Kenneth *Civilisation*, London 1971

Clark, Sir Kenneth *Female Beauty*, London & New York 1980

Colmer, Michael *Whalebone to See-through: A History of Body Packaging*, London 1979

Contini, Mila (translated by Olive Ordish) *5000 Years of Fashion*, New York 1979

Crawford, M D C *Philosophy in Clothing*, New York 1940

Dais, Celestine & Edward Lucie-Smith *How the Rich Lived 1870-1914*, London & New York 1976

Dars, Celestine *A Fashion Parade: The Seeberger Collection*, London 1979

Darwin, Charles *The Descent of Man*, London 1871

Delort, Robert (translated by Robert Allen) *Life in the Middle Ages*, New York 1973

Diamond, Milton *Sex Watching: Looking into the World of Sexual Behaviour*, London 1984

Hiler, Michael *Victorian Working Women: Portraits from Life*, London 1979

Hodgkin, Eliot *Fashion Drawing*, London 1932

Howell, Georgina (editor) *In Vogue: Six Decades of Fashion*, London 1975

Huet, Michel *The Dance, Art and Ritual of Africa*, London 1978

Hurlock, Elizabeth B *The Psychology of Dress*, New York 1929

Johanson, Donald C & Maitland A Edey *Lucy: The Beginnings of Mankind*, London 1981

Johnson, Virginia E, Robert C Kolodny & William H Master *Human Sexuality*, Boston 1982

Keenan, Brigid *The Women We Wanted to Look Like*, London 1977

Khornak, Lucille *Fashion 2001*, London 1982

Kirk, Kris & Ed Heath *Men In Frocks*, London 1984

Kirk, Malcolm *Man As Art: New Guinea Body Decoration*, London 1981

Kohler, Wolfgang *The Mentality of Apes*, London 1925

Koike, Kazuko (editor) *Issey Miyake: East Meets West*, Tokyo 1978

Kupfermann, Jeannette *The Ms Taken Body*, London 1979

LaVine, W Robert *In A Glamourous Fashion: The Fabulous Years of Hollywood Costume Design*, London 1980

Lacy, S & Don Morgan *Leg Art*, New Jersey 1981

Landley Moore, Doris *Fashion Through Fashion Plates*, London 1971

Landley Moore, Doris *The Women in Fashion*, London 1949

Langdale, Emile *Rose Bertin: The Creator of Fashion*, London 1913

Langdon-Davis *The Future of Nakedness*, New York, 1928

Langer, Lawrence *The Importance of Wearing Clothes*, London 1959

Laver, James *Taste and Fashion*, London 1975

Laver, James *Modesty of Dress*, London 1969

Laver, James *Costume and Fashion: A Concise History*, London 1982

Leakey, Richard E *The Making of Mankind*, London 1981

Luria, Gina & Virgia Tiger *Everywoman*, New York 1976

Lurie, Alison *The Language of Clothes*, New York 1981

Lynam, Ruth (editor) *Paris Fashion: The Great Designers and Their Creators*, London 1972

McClellan, Elizabeth *History of American Costume*, New York 1969

McDowell, Colin *McDowell's Directory of Twentieth Century Fashion*, London 1984

Mead, Margaret *Male and Female*, New York 1949

Morris, Desmond *The Naked Ape*, London 1969

Morris Desmond *Manwatching: A Field Guide to Human Behaviour*, London 1977

Morris, Desmond *Body Watching: A Field Guide to Human Behaviour*, London 1985

Oliver, William (editor) *The Handbook for Ladies' Maids and Guide to the Toilette*, London 1863

Orloff, Alexander *Carnival: Myth and Cult*, Wörgl, Austria 1981

Parker, Derek & Julia *The Natural History of the Chorus Girl*, Indianapolis 1975

Parson, Frank Alvah *Phsychology of Dress*, New York 1969

Pietropinto, Anthony & Jacqueline Simenauer *Beyond the Male Myth*, New York 1977

Platt, Colin *The Atlas of Medieval Man*, London 1979

Poiret, Paul *King of Fashion/My First Fifty Years*, Paris, London & Philadelphia 1931

Polemus, Ted & Lynn Proctor *Fashion and Anti-Fashion*, London 1978

Rattray Taylor G *Sex in History*, New York

Ratziel, F *The History of Mankind*, New York 1896

Reader, W J *Victorian England*, London 1974

Rennolds Milbank, Caroline *Couture: The Great Fashion Designers*, New York 1985

Richardson, Joanne *The Courtesans: The Demi-monde in 19th Century France*, London 1967

Richter, Stefan *Tattoo*, London & New York 1985

Riefenstahl, Leni *People of Kan*, London 1976

Robinson, Julian *The Golden Age of Style: Art Deco Fashion*, London, Paris & New York 1976

Rodofsky, Bernard *Are Clothes Modern?*, Chicago 1947

Rudofsky, Bernard *The Unfashionable Human Body*, London & New York 1972

Severin, Timothy *Vanishing Primitive Man*, New York 1973

Spencer, Charles *Erte*, London & New York, 1970

Squire, Geoffrey *Dress and Society 1560-1970*, New York 1974

Stein, Ralph *The Pin-Up from 1852 to Today*, Chicago 1974

Strong, Roy *Splendour at Court*, London 1973

Sutherland, Anne (editor) *Face Values*, London 1978

Tannahill, Reay *Sex in History*, London 1980

Thorndike Jr., Joseph J *The Very Rich: A History of Wealth*, New York 1980

Uzanne, Octave *The Frenchwoman of the Century*, Paris & London 1886

Veblen, Thorstein *Theory of The Leisure Class*, New York 1899

Virel, André (translated by I Mark) *Decorated Man: The Human Body as Art*, New York 1980

Waeehter, John *Man Before History*, London 1976

Waller, Jane (editor) *A Man's Book Fashion in the Man's World 1920-30s*, London 1977

Walz, Barbra & Bernadine Morris *The Fashion Makers*, New York 1978

Ward & Lock (publisher) *The Young Lady's Treasure Book and Guide to Fashion*, London 1883

Westermarck, E *History of Human Marriage*, London 1929

White, Palmer *Poiret*, London & New York 1973

Whittick, Arnold *Symbols, Signs and Their Meaning and Uses*, New York 1976

Willet Cunnington, C *Why Women Wear Clothes*, London 1949

Willet Cunnington, C *The History of Underclothes*, London 1951

Wilson, Elizabeth *Adorned in Dreams: Fashion and Modernity*, London 1985

Woolman Chase, Edna & Ilka Chase *Always in Vogue*, London 1954

Wortley, Richard *A Pictorial History of Striptease*, London 1976

Wright, Thomas *Womankind In Western Europe*, London 1869

York, Peter *Style Wars*, London 1980

Yowall, H W *A Fashion of Life*, London 1966